Presidential Powers

Other Books of Related Interest:

Opposing Viewpoints Series

Privacy

At Issue Series

Does the U.S. Two-Party System Still Work?

Current Controversies Series

Torture

"Congress shall make
no law ... abridging
the freedom of speech,
or of the press."

First Amendment to the U.S. Constitution

The basic foundation of our democracy is the First Amendment guarantee of freedom of expression. The Opposing Viewpoints Series is dedicated to the concept of this basic freedom and the idea that it is more important to practice it than to enshrine it.

OPPOSING
VIEWPOINTS®
SERIES

Presidential Powers

Noah Berlatsky, Book Editor

GREENHAVEN PRESS
A part of Gale, Cengage Learning

GALE
CENGAGE Learning™

Detroit • New York • San Francisco • New Haven, Conn • Waterville, Maine • London

GALE
CENGAGE Learning™

Christine Nasso, *Publisher*
Elizabeth Des Chenes, *Managing Editor*

LIBRARY OF CONGRESS CATALOGING-IN-PUBLICATION DATA

Presidential powers / Noah Berlatsky, book editor.
  p. cm. -- (Opposing viewpoints)
  Includes bibliographical references and index.
  ISBN 978-0-7377-4982-3 (hardcover) -- ISBN 978-0-7377-4983-0 (pbk.)
  1. Executive power--United States--Juvenile literature. 2. Presidents--United States--Juvenile literature. I. Berlatsky, Noah.
  JK517.P74 2010
  352.23'50973--dc22

                                                          2009054109

Contents

Chapter 3: To What Extent Should the President Be Constrained by Domestic Law?

Chapter 4: Is the President Bound by International Law?

Why Consider Opposing Viewpoints?

> *"The only way in which a human being can make some approach to knowing the whole of a subject is by hearing what can be said about it by persons of every variety of opinion and studying all modes in which it can be looked at by every character of mind. No wise man ever acquired his wisdom in any mode but this."*
>
> *John Stuart Mill*

In our media-intensive culture it is not difficult to find differing opinions. Thousands of newspapers and magazines and dozens of radio and television talk shows resound with differing points of view. The difficulty lies in deciding which opinion to agree with and which "experts" seem the most credible. The more inundated we become with differing opinions and claims, the more essential it is to hone critical reading and thinking skills to evaluate these ideas. Opposing Viewpoints books address this problem directly by presenting stimulating debates that can be used to enhance and teach these skills. The varied opinions contained in each book examine many different aspects of a single issue. While examining these conveniently edited opposing views, readers can develop critical thinking skills such as the ability to compare and contrast authors' credibility, facts, argumentation styles, use of persuasive techniques, and other stylistic tools. In short, the Opposing Viewpoints Series is an ideal way to attain the higher-level thinking and reading skills so essential in a culture of diverse and contradictory opinions.

In addition to providing a tool for critical thinking, Opposing Viewpoints books challenge readers to question their own strongly held opinions and assumptions. Most people form their opinions on the basis of upbringing, peer pressure, and personal, cultural, or professional bias. By reading carefully balanced opposing views, readers must directly confront new ideas as well as the opinions of those with whom they disagree. This is not to simplistically argue that everyone who reads opposing views will—or should—change his or her opinion. Instead, the series enhances readers' understanding of their own views by encouraging confrontation with opposing ideas. Careful examination of others' views can lead to the readers' understanding of the logical inconsistencies in their own opinions, perspective on why they hold an opinion, and the consideration of the possibility that their opinion requires further evaluation.

Evaluating Other Opinions

To ensure that this type of examination occurs, Opposing Viewpoints books present all types of opinions. Prominent spokespeople on different sides of each issue as well as well-known professionals from many disciplines challenge the reader. An additional goal of the series is to provide a forum for other, less known, or even unpopular viewpoints. The opinion of an ordinary person who has had to make the decision to cut off life support from a terminally ill relative, for example, may be just as valuable and provide just as much insight as a medical ethicist's professional opinion. The editors have two additional purposes in including these less known views. One, the editors encourage readers to respect others' opinions—even when not enhanced by professional credibility. It is only by reading or listening to and objectively evaluating others' ideas that one can determine whether they are worthy of consideration. Two, the inclusion of such viewpoints encourages the important critical thinking skill of objectively evaluating an author's credentials and bias. This evaluation will illuminate an author's reasons for taking a particular stance on an issue and will aid in readers' evaluation of the author's ideas.

It is our hope that these books will give readers a deeper understanding of the issues debated and an appreciation of the complexity of even seemingly simple issues when good and honest people disagree. This awareness is particularly important in a democratic society such as ours in which people enter into public debate to determine the common good. Those with whom one disagrees should not be regarded as enemies but rather as people whose views deserve careful examination and may shed light on one's own.

Thomas Jefferson once said that "difference of opinion leads to inquiry, and inquiry to truth." Jefferson, a broadly educated man, argued that "if a nation expects to be ignorant and free ... it expects what never was and never will be." As individuals and as a nation, it is imperative that we consider the opinions of others and examine them with skill and discernment. The Opposing Viewpoints Series is intended to help readers achieve this goal.

David L. Bender and Bruno Leone,
Founders

Introduction

"There will be a full accounting for the cruel and disgraceful abuse of Iraqi detainees. . . . Those responsible for these abuses have caused harm that goes well beyond the walls of a prison."

—President George W. Bush, May 10, 2004, responding to revelations of abuses of detainees at Abu Ghraib prison in Iraq

Some of the most disturbing and controversial arguments around presidential and executive power in recent years have involved the issue of torture—and especially the use of torture at the Abu Ghraib detention center in Iraq.

Iraqi prisoners were held by American forces at Abu Ghraib following the U.S. invasion of Iraq in 2003. In 2004, several news sites began reporting that serious abuses had occurred in the prison, including physical and psychological torture, sexual abuse of prisoners, and even homicide of prisoners. Graphic photographs were made public showing naked prisoners being abused and tortured.

The George W. Bush administration condemned the actions at Abu Ghraib. Secretary of Defense Donald Rumsfeld called the actions "totally unacceptable and un-American," and promised to "hold accountable" those responsible for the abuses, according to a May 5, 2004, article on *Foxnews.com*. A number of soldiers were, in fact, dishonorably discharged for their roles in the abuses. A commanding officer was demoted, and two soldiers were sentenced to prison.

However, some critics have argued that the guards who committed the abuses were, in fact, acting under orders from the chain of command, and ultimately from administration officials. The convicted soldiers themselves have argued that in carrying out torture and abuse of detainees they were actually following orders. As evidence, lawyers for the convicted soldiers have pointed to Department of Justice (DOJ) memos written before the abuses but only released to the public in 2009. Tim Reid, writing in the London *Times* online on May 2, 2009, reported that "the memos showed that the harsh interrogation tactics were approved and authorised at the highest levels of the White House." In other words, tactics such as the use of dogs to terrorize prisoners, slamming prisoners into walls, and waterboarding (a torture technique that involves controlled drowning) were all approved by government lawyers before they were used on prisoners at Abu Ghraib.

A Congressional investigation into Abu Ghraib released in 2008 also concluded that executive department officials were ultimately responsible for many of the abuses. The Senate Armed Services Committee concluded that "Interrogation techniques such as stripping detainees of their clothes, placing them in stress positions and using military working dogs to intimidate them appeared in Iraq only after they had been approved" in the 2001 U.S. invasion of Afghanistan, and at the prison in Guantanamo Bay, Cuba, where many terrorist suspects were held. The report linked the abuses at Abu Ghraib to actions taken by Defense Secretary Rumsfeld. It also implicated President George W. Bush, who signed a memorandum stating that the Geneva Conventions, the international laws of war, did not apply to terrorist detainees. "The president's order closed off application of Common Article 3 of the Geneva Conventions, which would have afforded minimum standards for humane treatment," according to the Congressional report.

Several commentators argued that because the Department of Justice had approved certain kinds of torture, those who relied on that approval and who tortured prisoners should not face prosecution. In an editorial on July 27, 2009, for example, the *Washington Post* argued that Attorney General Eric Holder was right to "shield . . . from criminal prosecution" interrogators who acted in good faith. The *Post* argued, however, that those who went "beyond" what the Department of Justice sanctioned should be prosecuted. Thus, for the *Post*, the soldiers who committed the worst abuses at Abu Ghraib, such as actually torturing prisoners to death, deserved prosecution, because killing prisoners was not authorized by the Justice Department.

Glenn Greenwald writing for Salon.com disagreed strongly with the *Post's* assessment. "We now apparently believe," Greenwald noted sarcastically, "that Presidents are free to break the law as long as they can find a low-level DOJ functionary to write a memo justifying that conduct in advance." For Greenwald, the main crime was the authorization of torture in the first place. If high-level executives are not held accountable for abusive policies, Greenwald argued, then "Presidents are literally no longer bound by the rule of law."

The articles in *Opposing Viewpoints: Presidential Powers* discuss the same issues of executive power and abuse that were debated following the revelations at Abu Ghraib. The chapters address the questions: Should the President Have the Power to Order Torture? How Much Power Should the President Have to Operate in Secret? To What Extent Should the President Be Constrained by Domestic Law? and Is the President Bound by International Law? Each of the following viewpoints attempts to find a balance between national security and civil liberties, and between the power of the presidency and the rule of law.

OPPOSING
VIEWPOINTS®
SERIES

CHAPTER 1

Should the President Have the Power to Order Torture?

Chapter Preface

The question of whether the president can order torture, in practice, often turns into a question about what torture is. For example, can the president or the executive branch order prisoners to be stripped naked? Can prisoners be prevented from going to sleep? And are these practices torture?

One of the most controversial techniques used by the George W. Bush administration on some terrorist suspects was known as "waterboarding." Brian Ross and Richard Esposito described waterboarding in a November 18, 2005, *ABC News* article as follows: "The prisoner is bound to an inclined board, feet raised and head slightly below the feet. Cellophane is wrapped over the prisoner's face and water is poured over him. Unavoidably, the gag reflex kicks in and a terrifying fear of drowning leads to almost instant pleas to bring the treatment to a halt."

Some commentators have argued that waterboarding is not an especially harsh punishment. For example, Joseph Farah writing on January 2, 2009, on *WorldNetDaily* noted that waterboarding is used on U.S. troops to prepare them to withstand enemy interrogation. He then asked disbelievingly how it could be "OK for us to do this to America's best and brightest but it's too horrible for our worst enemies?" Similarly, when asked by conservative radio show host Scott Hennen if "a dunk in water is a no-brainer if it can save lives?" then Vice President Richard (Dick) Cheney responded, "It's a no-brainer for me," as reported by Mark Tran in the *Guardian* on October 27, 2006. Cheney later admitted explicitly that the United States had waterboarded terror suspects, and he argued that the waterboarding had resulted in valuable intelligence. In particular, Cheney acknowledged that Khalid Sheikh Mohammed, an al-Qaeda operative involved in repeated attacks on the United States, was waterboarded 183 times while in U.S.

custody. Cheney said that this effort was a "success" and that the United States gained vital information from Mohammed, according to James Gordon Meek writing in the *New York Daily News* on April 22, 2009.

In that same article, however, Meek quotes an intelligence source as stating, "Cheney is full of crap," because no useful intelligence was gained from waterboarding Mohammed. Moreover, many commentaters have argued that waterboarding is, in fact, torture. Christopher Hitchens, a supporter of the Iraq war and of many George W. Bush administration policies, allowed himself to be waterboarded. Describing the sensation in an August 2008 *Vanity Fair* article, he stated, "You may have read by now the official lie about this treatment, which is that it 'simulates' the feeling of drowning. This is not the case. You feel that you are drowning because you *are* drowning. . . ." He added that "if waterboarding does not constitute torture, then there is no such thing as torture." Similarly, conservative radio host Erich "Mancow" Muller agreed to be waterboarded in order to prove that the practice was not torture. Instead, after being waterboarded, he too concluded that the treatment was "absolutely torture" according to an account on May 22, 2009, in the *Huffington Post*.

In a press conference in April 2009, President Barack Obama said, "I believe that waterboarding was torture and, whatever legal rational[e]s were used, it was a mistake," according to a report by Ewen MacAskill in the *Guardian*. However, while Obama appears to have put an end to the practice by the United States, other questions about the use of torture, in the past and the future, continue to be vigorously debated, as the following viewpoints make clear.

> *"To call this a program of torture is to libel the dedicated professionals who have saved American lives. . . . To completely rule out enhanced interrogation methods in the future . . . would make the American people less safe."*

Enhanced Interrogation Helps Keep America Safe

Richard B. Cheney

Richard B. "Dick" Cheney was vice president of the United States during the administration of President George W. Bush. In the following viewpoint, he argues that the Bush administration's use of enhanced interrogation techniques was a necessary response to the threat of future terrorist attacks after September 11, 2001. Cheney states that enhanced interrogation was used only on the most dangerous terrorists, and that it provided important information. He argues that the use of such methods helped to prevent terrorist attacks after 9/11, and suggests that abandoning these methods places the United States at risk.

Richard B. Cheney, "Remarks by Richard B. Cheney," *American Enterprise Institute*, May 21, 2009. Reproduced by permission.

As you read, consider the following questions:

1. According to Dick Cheney, what serious blows against enemy operations did the administration strike?

2. How many terrorists were subjected to waterboarding, according to Cheney?

3. What are the true sources of resentment that cause terrorists to attack America, in Cheney's view?

Right now there is considerable debate in this city [Washington, D.C.] about the measures our administration [the George W. Bush administration, in which Cheney was vice president] took to defend the American people. Today I want to set forth the strategic thinking behind our policies. I do so as one who was there every day of the Bush administration, who supported the policies when they were made, and without hesitation would do so again in the same circumstances. . . .

Reacting to 9/11

Our administration always faced its share of criticism, and from some quarters it was always intense. That was especially so in the later years of our term, when the dangers were as serious as ever, but the sense of general alarm after September 11, 2001, was a fading memory. Part of our responsibility, as we saw it, was not to forget the terrible harm that had been done to America . . . and not to let 9/11 become the prelude to something much bigger and far worse.

That attack itself was, of course, the most devastating strike in a series of terrorist plots carried out against Americans at home and abroad. In 1993, terrorists bombed the World Trade Center, hoping to bring down the towers with a blast from below. The attacks continued in 1995, with the bombing of U.S. facilities in Riyadh, Saudi Arabia; the killing of servicemen at Khobar Towers [in Saudi Arabia] in 1996;

the attack on our embassies in East Africa in 1998; the murder of American sailors on the *USS Cole* in 2000; and then the hijackings of 9/11, and all the grief and loss we suffered on that day.

9/11 caused everyone to take a serious second look at threats that had been gathering for a while, and enemies whose plans were getting bolder and more sophisticated. Throughout the [19]90s, America had responded to these attacks, if at all, on an ad hoc basis. The first attack on the World Trade Center was treated as a law enforcement problem, with everything handled after the fact—crime scene, arrests, indictments, convictions, prison sentences, case closed.

That's how it seemed from a law enforcement perspective, at least—but for the terrorists the case was not closed. For them, it was another offensive strike in their ongoing war against the United States. And it turned their minds to even harder strikes with higher casualties. 9/11 made necessary a shift of policy, aimed at a clear strategic threat—what the Congress called "an unusual and extraordinary threat to the national security and foreign policy of the United States." From that moment forward, instead of merely preparing to round up the suspects and count up the victims after the next attack, we were determined to prevent attacks in the first place.

We could count on almost universal support back then, because everyone understood the environment we were in. We'd just been hit by a foreign enemy—leaving 3,000 Americans dead, more than we lost at Pearl Harbor [more than 2,400 Americans died in the Japanese attack on Pearl Harbor, Hawaii, on December 7, 1941]. In Manhattan, we were staring at 16 acres of ashes. The Pentagon took a direct hit, and the Capitol or the White House were spared only by the Americans on Flight 93, who died bravely and defiantly.[1]

1. On September 11, terrorists flew a plane into the Pentagon as well as into the World Trade Center. A third hijacked plane crash landed in Pennsylvania when passengers attacked the hijackers.

Everyone expected a follow-on attack, and our job was to stop it. We didn't know what was coming next, but everything we did know in that autumn of 2001 looked bad. This was the world in which al-Qaeda [terrorist group responsible for September 11, 2001, attacks] was seeking nuclear technology, and A.Q. Khan[2] was selling nuclear technology on the black market. We had the anthrax attack from an unknown source.[3] We had the training camps of Afghanistan, and dictators like Saddam Hussein [of Iraq] with known ties to Mideast terrorists.

These are just a few of the problems we had on our hands. And foremost on our minds was the prospect of the very worst coming to pass—a 9/11 with nuclear weapons. . . .

Never Again

To make certain our nation never again faced such a day of horror, we developed a comprehensive strategy, beginning with far greater homeland security to make the United States a harder target. But since wars cannot be won on the defensive, we moved decisively against the terrorists in their hideouts and sanctuaries, and committed to using every asset to take down their networks. We decided, as well, to confront the regimes that sponsored terrorists, and to go after those who provide sanctuary, funding, and weapons to enemies of the United States. We turned special attention to regimes that had the capacity to build weapons of mass destruction, and might transfer such weapons to terrorists.

We did all of these things, and with bipartisan support put all these policies in place. It has resulted in serious blows against enemy operations: the take-down of the A.Q. Khan network and the dismantling of Libya's nuclear program. It's required the commitment of many thousands of troops in

2. Abdul Qadeer Khan, a Pakistani nuclear scientist who was involved in illegally disseminating nuclear technology.
3. In September 2001 letters containing deadly anthrax spores were mailed to news media outlets and to several Democratic senators.

two theaters of war, with high points and some low points in both Iraq and Afghanistan—and at every turn, the people of our military carried the heaviest burden. Well over seven years into the effort, one thing we know is that the enemy has spent most of this time on the defensive—and every attempt to strike inside the United States has failed.

So we're left to draw one of two conclusions—and here is the great dividing line in our current debate over national security. You can look at the facts and conclude that the comprehensive strategy has worked, and therefore needs to be continued as vigilantly as ever. Or you can look at the same set of facts and conclude that 9/11 was a one-off event—coordinated, devastating, but also unique and not sufficient to justify a sustained wartime effort. Whichever conclusion you arrive at, it will shape your entire view of the last seven years, and of the policies necessary to protect America for years to come.

Executive Powers

The key to any strategy is accurate intelligence, and skilled professionals to get that information in time to use it. In seeking to guard this nation against the threat of catastrophic violence, our Administration gave intelligence officers the tools and lawful authority they needed to gain vital information. We didn't invent that authority. It is drawn from Article Two of the Constitution.[4] And it was given specificity by the Congress after 9/11, in a Joint Resolution authorizing "all necessary and appropriate force" to protect the American people.

Our government prevented attacks and saved lives through the Terrorist Surveillance Program,[5] which let us intercept calls and track contacts between al-Qaeda operatives and persons inside the United States. The program was top secret,

4. Article 2 is the part of the Constitution that covers the Executive Branch, including the president.
5. The Terrorist Surveillance Program allowed the National Security Agency to monitor phone calls without a warrant.

and for good reason, until the editors of the *New York Times* got it and put it on the front page. After 9/11, the *Times* had spent months publishing the pictures and the stories of everyone killed by al-Qaeda on 9/11. Now here was that same newspaper publishing secrets in a way that could only help al-Qaeda. It impressed the Pulitzer committee, but it damn sure didn't serve the interests of our country, or the safety of our people.

In the years after 9/11, our government also understood that the safety of the country required collecting information known only to the worst of the terrorists. And in a few cases, that information could be gained only through tough interrogations.

In top secret meetings about enhanced interrogations, I made my own beliefs clear. I was and remain a strong proponent of our enhanced interrogation program. The interrogations were used on hardened terrorists after other efforts failed. They were legal, essential, justified, successful, and the right thing to do. The intelligence officers who questioned the terrorists can be proud of their work and proud of the results, because they prevented the violent death of thousands, if not hundreds of thousands, of innocent people.

Our successors in office have their own views on all of these matters.

By presidential decision, last month [March 2009] we saw the selective release of documents relating to enhanced interrogations. This is held up as a bold exercise in open government, honoring the public's right to know. We're informed, as well, that there was much agonizing over this decision.

Valuable Information Was Gained

Yet somehow, when the soul-searching was done and the veil was lifted on the policies of the Bush administration, the public was given less than half the truth. The released memos were carefully redacted to leave out references to what our government learned through the methods in question. Other memos, laying out specific terrorist plots that were averted, apparently were not even considered for release. For reasons the administration has yet to explain, they believe the public has a right to know the method of the questions, but not the content of the answers.

Over on the left wing of the president's party, there appears to be little curiosity in finding out what was learned from the terrorists. The kind of answers they're after would be heard before a so-called "Truth Commission."[6] Some are even demanding that those who recommended and approved the interrogations be prosecuted, in effect treating political disagreements as a punishable offense, and political opponents as criminals. It's hard to imagine a worse precedent, filled with more possibilities for trouble and abuse, than to have an incoming administration criminalize the policy decisions of its predecessors.

Apart from doing a serious injustice to intelligence operators and lawyers who deserve far better for their devoted service, the danger here is a loss of focus on national security, and what it requires. I would advise the administration to think very carefully about the course ahead. All the zeal that has been directed at interrogations is utterly misplaced. And staying on that path will only lead our government further away from its duty to protect the American people.

One person who by all accounts objected to the release of the interrogation memos was the Director of Central Intelligence, Leon Panetta. He was joined in that view by at least four of his predecessors. I assume they felt this way because they understand the importance of protecting intelligence sources, methods, and personnel. But now that this once top-secret information is out for all to see—including the en-

6. A commission set up to investigate human rights abuses.

emy—let me draw your attention to some points that are routinely overlooked.

It is a fact that only detainees of the highest intelligence value were ever subjected to enhanced interrogation. You've heard endlessly about waterboarding.[7] It happened to three terrorists. One of them was Khalid Sheikh Muhammed—the mastermind of 9/11, who has also boasted about beheading Daniel Pearl.[8]

We had a lot of blind spots after the attacks on our country. We didn't know about al-Qaeda's plans, but Khalid Sheikh Muhammed [KSM] and a few others did know. And with many thousands of innocent lives potentially in the balance, we didn't think it made sense to let the terrorists answer questions in their own good time, if they answered them at all.

Maybe you've heard that when we captured KSM, he said he would talk as soon as he got to New York City and saw his lawyer. But like many critics of interrogations, he clearly misunderstood the business at hand. American personnel were not there to commence an elaborate legal proceeding, but to extract information from him before al-Qaeda could strike again and kill more of our people.

Not Abu Ghraib

In public discussion of these matters, there has been a strange and sometimes willful attempt to conflate what happened at Abu Ghraib prison with the top secret program of enhanced interrogations.[9] At Abu Ghraib, a few sadistic prison guards abused inmates in violation of American law, military regulations, and simple decency. For the harm they did, to Iraqi

7. Waterboarding is a torture method in which the victim has water poured into his airway, effectively drowning him for brief periods.
8. Khalid Sheikh Muhammed is a member of the al-Qaida terrorist network. He is believed to have been involved in numerous terrorist actions, including the 2002 kidnapping and murder of journalist Daniel Pearl.
9. At Abu Ghraib prison in Iraq, American personnel tortured, raped, and murdered prisoners. The abuses occurred following the U.S. invasion of Iraq in 2003, and became public in 2004.

prisoners and to America's cause, they deserved and received Army justice. And it takes a deeply unfair cast of mind to equate the disgraces of Abu Ghraib with the lawful, skillful, and entirely honorable work of CIA personnel trained to deal with a few malevolent men.

Even before the interrogation program began, and throughout its operation, it was closely reviewed to ensure that every method used was in full compliance with the Constitution, statutes, and treaty obligations. On numerous occasions, leading members of Congress, including the current speaker of the House, were briefed on the program and on the methods.

Yet for all these exacting efforts to do a hard and necessary job and to do it right, we hear from some quarters nothing but feigned outrage based on a false narrative. In my long experience in Washington, few matters have inspired so much contrived indignation and phony moralizing as the interrogation methods applied to a few captured terrorists.

I might add that people who consistently distort the truth in this way are in no position to lecture anyone about "values." Intelligence officers of the United States were not trying to rough up some terrorists simply to avenge the dead of 9/11. We know the difference in this country between justice and vengeance. Intelligence officers were not trying to get terrorists to confess to past killings; they were trying to prevent future killings. From the beginning of the program, there was only one focused and all-important purpose. We sought, and we in fact obtained, specific information on terrorist plans.

Those are the basic facts on enhanced interrogations. And to call this a program of torture is to libel the dedicated professionals who have saved American lives, and to cast terrorists and murderers as innocent victims. What's more, to completely rule out enhanced interrogation methods in the future is unwise in the extreme. It is recklessness cloaked in righteousness, and would make the American people less safe.

Cheney Pushed for Enhanced Interrogation

Shortly after the first accused terrorists reached the U.S. naval prison at Guantanamo Bay, Cuba, on Jan. 11, 2002, a delegation from CIA [Central Intelligence Agency] headquarters arrived in the Situation Room. The agency presented a delicate problem to White House counsel Alberto R. Gonzales, a man with next to no experience on the subject. Vice President [Dick] Cheney's lawyer, who had a great deal of experience, sat nearby.

The meeting marked "the first time that the issue of interrogations comes up" among top-ranking White House officials, recalled John C. Yoo, who represented the Justice Department. "The CIA guys said, 'We're going to have some real difficulties getting actionable intelligence from detainees'" if interrogators confined themselves to treatment allowed by the Geneva Conventions.

From that moment, well before previous accounts have suggested. Cheney turned his attention to the practical business of crushing a captive's will to resist. The vice president's office played a central role in shattering limits on coercion of prisoners in U.S. custody, commissioning and defending legal opinions that the [George W.] Bush administration has since portrayed as the initiatives, months later, of lower-ranking officials. . . .

Barton Gellman and Jo Becker,
"Pushing the Envelope on Presidential Power," Washington Post,
June 25, 2007. http://voices.washingtonpost.com.

Do Not Blame America

Another term out there that slipped into the discussion is the notion that American interrogation practices were a "recruit ment tool" for the enemy. On this theory, by the tough questioning of killers, we have supposedly fallen short of our own values. This recruitment-tool theory has become something of a mantra lately, including from the President [Barack Obama] himself. And after a familiar fashion, it excuses the violent and blames America for the evil that others do. It's another version of that same old refrain from the Left, "We brought it on ourselves."

It is much closer to the truth that terrorists hate this country precisely because of the values we profess and seek to live by, not by some alleged failure to do so. Nor are terrorists or those who see them as victims exactly the best judges of America's moral standards, one way or the other.

Critics of our policies are given to lecturing on the theme of being consistent with American values. But no moral value held dear by the American people obliges public servants ever to sacrifice innocent lives to spare a captured terrorist from unpleasant things. And when an entire population is targeted by a terror network, nothing is more consistent with American values than to stop them.

As a practical matter, too, terrorists may lack much, but they have never lacked for grievances against the United States. Our belief in freedom of speech and religion, our belief in equal rights for women, our support for Israel, our cultural and political influence in the world—these are the true sources of resentment, all mixed in with the lies and conspiracy theories of the radical clerics. These recruitment tools were in vigorous use throughout the 1990s, and they were sufficient to motivate the nineteen recruits who boarded those planes on September 11, 2001.

The United States of America was a good country before 9/11, just as we are today. List all the things that make us a force for good in the world—for liberty, for human rights, for the rational, peaceful resolution of differences—and what you end up with is a list of the reasons why the terrorists hate

America. If fine speech-making, appeals to reason, or pleas for compassion had the power to move them, the terrorists would long ago have abandoned the field. And when they see the American government caught up in arguments about interrogations, or whether foreign terrorists have constitutional rights, they don't stand back in awe of our legal system and wonder whether they had misjudged us all along. Instead the terrorists see just what they were hoping for—our unity gone, our resolve shaken, our leaders distracted. In short, they see weakness and opportunity.

What is equally certain is this: The broad-based strategy set in motion by President [George W.] Bush obviously had nothing to do with causing the events of 9/11. But the serious way we dealt with terrorists from then on, and all the intelligence we gathered in that time, had everything to do with preventing another 9/11 on our watch. The enhanced interrogations of high-value detainees and the terrorist surveillance program have without question made our country safer. Every senior official who has been briefed on these classified matters knows of specific attacks that were in the planning stages and were stopped by the programs we put in place.

This might explain why President Obama has reserved unto himself the right to order the use of enhanced interrogation should he deem it appropriate. What value remains to that authority is debatable, given that the enemy now knows exactly what interrogation methods to train against, and which ones not to worry about. Yet having reserved for himself the authority to order enhanced interrogation after an emergency, you would think that President Obama would be less disdainful of what his predecessor authorized after 9/11. It's almost gone unnoticed that the president has retained the power to order the same methods in the same circumstances. When they talk about interrogations, he and his administration speak as if they have resolved some great moral dilemma in how to extract critical information from terrorists. Instead they have put the decision off, while assigning a presumption of moral superiority to any decision they make in the future.

Focus on the Terrorists

Releasing the interrogation memos was flatly contrary to the national security interest of the United States. The harm done only begins with top secret information now in the hands of the terrorists, who have just received a lengthy insert for their training manual. Across the world, governments that have helped us capture terrorists will fear that sensitive joint operations will be compromised. And at the CIA, operatives are left to wonder if they can depend on the White House or Congress to back them up when the going gets tough. Why should any agency employee take on a difficult assignment when, even though they act lawfully and in good faith, years down the road the press and Congress will treat everything they do with suspicion, outright hostility, and second-guessing? Some members of Congress are notorious for demanding they be briefed into the most sensitive intelligence programs. They support them in private, and then head for the hills at the first sign of controversy.

As far as the interrogations are concerned, all that remains an official secret is the information we gained as a result. Some of his [President Obama's] defenders say the unseen memos are inconclusive, which only raises the question why they won't let the American people decide that for themselves. I saw that information as vice president, and I reviewed some of it again at the National Archives last month. I've formally asked that it be declassified so the American people can see the intelligence we obtained, the things we learned, and the consequences for national security. And as you may have heard, last week [May 2009] that request was formally rejected. It's worth recalling that ultimate power of declassification belongs to the President himself. President Obama has used his declassification power to reveal what happened in the interrogation of terrorists. Now let him use that same power to show Americans what did not happen, thanks to the good work of our intelligence officials.

I believe this information will confirm the value of inter-rogations—and I am not alone. President Obama's own Di-rector of National Intelligence, Admiral [Dennis C.] Blair, has put it this way: "High value information came from interroga-tions in which those methods were used and provided a deeper understanding of the al-Qaeda organization that was attacking this country." End quote. Admiral Blair put that conclusion in writing, only to see it mysteriously deleted in a later version released by the administration—the missing twenty-six words that tell an inconvenient truth. But they couldn't change the words of George Tenet, the CIA Director under Presidents [Bill] Clinton and Bush, who bluntly said: "I know that this program has saved lives. I know we've disrupted plots. I know this program alone is worth more than the FBI, the Central Intelligence Agency, and the National Security Agency put to-gether have been able to tell us."

If Americans do get the chance to learn what our country was spared, it'll do more than clarify the urgency and the rightness of enhanced interrogations in the years after 9/11. It may help us to stay focused on dangers that have not gone away. Instead of idly debating which political opponents to prosecute and punish, our attention will return to where it belongs—on the continuing threat of terrorist violence, and on stopping the men who are planning it.

> *"As we slide down the slippery slope to torture in general, we should also realize that there is a chasm at the bottom called extrajudicial execution."*

Torture Does Not Make America Safer

Alfred W. McCoy

Alfred W. McCoy is a professor of history at the University of Wisconsin-Madison and author of A Question of Torture: CIA Interrogation, from the Cold War to the War on Terror. *In the following viewpoint, he argues that using torture does not protect America. In the first place, he notes that the ticking time bomb scenario is extremely improbable. Further, he argues, torture is itself a very poor way to get information, because victims either resist or blurt out anything to stop the pain. Finally, he says, torture undermines a regime's legitimacy in the eyes of both its enemies and its own people.*

As you read, consider the following questions:

1. Why did President George W. Bush say that he could not reveal the specific methods used in Central Intelligence Agency interrogations?

Alfred W. McCoy, "The Myth of the Ticking Time Bomb," *The Progressive*, October 2006. Reproduced by permission of *The Progressive*, 409 East Main St., Madison, WI 53703, www.progressive.org.

2. According to Alfred W. McCoy, trained interrogators perform within what range when separating truth from lies?

3. McCoy says that limited surgical torture is useless, but what other kind of torture does he say can produce useful intelligence?

Ask not for whom the bomb ticks, Mr. and Ms. America. Right now, across Los Angeles, timers on dozens of toxic nerve-gas canisters are set to detonate in just hours and send some two million Americans to their deaths in writhing agony.

But take hope. We have one chance, just one, to avert this atrocity and save the lives of millions. Agent Jack Bauer of the Counter Terrorist Unit has his hunting knife poised over the eye of a trembling traitor who may know the identity of those who set these bombs. As a clock ticks menacingly and the camera focuses on knife point poised to plunge into eyeball, the traitor breaks and identifies the Muslim terrorists, giving Agent Bauer the lead he needs to crack this case wide open.

As happens with mind-numbing regularity every week on Fox Television's hit show *24*, torture has once again worked to save us all from the terror of a ticking bomb, affirming for millions of loyal viewers that torture is a necessary weapon in [President] George [W.] Bush's war on terror. . . .

Bush as Jack Bauer

Just days before the fifth anniversary of 9/11 [the terrorist attacks of September 11, 2001], President Bush himself appeared live from the East Room before an audience of handpicked 9/11 families for a dramatic announcement that mimed, with eerie precision, the ticking-bomb logic of *24*, which is wildly popular among Washington's neoconservatives.[1] With clipped, secret-agent diction reminiscent of the

---

1. Neoconservatives are a political faction which generally advocates aggressive use of force to counter terrorist and other threats to the United States.

show's Emmy Award-winning star, Kiefer Sutherland, Bush said he was transferring fourteen top Al Qaeda captives, including the alleged 9/11 mastermind, Khalid Sheik Mohammed, from long-secret CIA [Central Intelligence Agency] prisons to Guantánamo Bay.[2] At once both repudiating and legitimating past abuses, Bush denied that he had ever authorized "torture." Simultaneously, he defended the CIA's effort to coerce "vital information" from these "dangerous" captives with what the President called an "alternative set of procedures"—a euphemism transparent to any viewer of *24*.

In defense of the CIA's past and future use of this "alternative set of procedures," Bush told his national television audience a thrilling tale of covert action derring-do almost plucked from the pages of a script for *24*. After "they risked their lives to capture some of the most brutal terrorists on Earth," courageous American agents "worked day and night" to track down "a trusted associate of [al Qaeda leader] Osama bin Laden" named Abu Zubaydah. But once in custody, he was "defiant and evasive." Knowing that "captured terrorists have . . . intelligence that cannot be found any other place," the CIA, with White House approval, applied that "alternative set of procedures" and thereby extracted timely information that "helped in the planning . . . of the operation that captured Khalid Sheik Mohammed [KSM]." Then, "KSM was questioned by the CIA using these procedures," producing intelligence that stopped a succession of lethal ticking bombs.

The mind-boggling catalogue of these plots, the President told us, included "Al Qaeda's efforts to produce anthrax," a terror assault on U.S. Marines in Djibouti [the Republic of Djibouti is in the Horn of Africa] with "an explosive-laden water tanker," "a planned attack on the U.S. consulate in Karachi [the largest city in Pakistan] using car bombs," "a plot to hijack passenger planes and fly them into Heathrow [airport

2. Guantánamo Bay in Cuba is the site of a U.S. detention camp that holds many alleged terrorists.

in London]," and "planned attacks on buildings in the United States" with bombs planted "to prevent the people trapped above from escaping out the windows."

Of course, the President could not, he said with a knowing wink to his audience, describe "the specific methods used in these CIA interrogations" because "it would help the terrorists learn how to resist questioning." Although these "procedures were tough," they had proved vital, the President assured us, in extracting "information about terrorist plans we could not get anywhere else" and thus prevented Al Qaeda from "launching another attack against the American homeland." If Congress and the Supreme Court would simply set aside their constitutional qualms about these "tough" methods, Bush concluded, then the "brave men and women" who work in this CIA program can continue "to obtain information that will save innocent lives."

The Ticking Time Bomb Scenario

As in so many of these ticking-bomb tales, Bush's supposed successes crumble on closer examination. Just four days later, *The New York Times* reported that the FBI [Federal Bureau of Investigation] claimed it got the key information from Abu Zubaydah with its noncoercive methods and that other agencies already had much of his supposedly "vital" intelligence.

Like President Bush, influential pro-pain pundits have long cited the ticking-bomb scenario to defend torture as a necessary evil in the war on terror. Indeed, in this most pragmatic of modern societies, we are witnessing a rare triumph of academic philosophy in the realm of national security.

More than thirty years ago, the philosopher Michael Walzer, writing about the ancient problem of "dirty hands" for an obscure academic journal, *Philosophy and Public Affairs*, speculated about the morality of a politician "asked to authorize the torture of a captured rebel leader who knows the locality of a number of bombs hidden in apartment buildings around the city, set to go off within the next *twenty-four hours.*" [Emphasis added.] Even though he believes torture is "wrong, indeed abominable," this moral politician orders the man tortured, "convinced that he must do so for the sake of the people who might otherwise die in the explosions."

In all likelihood, Walzer's writing would have remained unnoticed on page 167 of an unread journal if not for the tireless efforts of an academic acolyte, Alan Dershowitz of Harvard Law School. In newspaper op-eds and television appearances since 9/11, Dershowitz has transformed this fragmentary philosophical rumination into a full-blown case for torture by recounting a similar scenario which, often set in Times Square, "involves a captured terrorist who refuses to divulge information about the imminent use of weapons of mass destruction, such as a nuclear, chemical, or biological device, that are capable of killing and injuring thousands of civilians."

From this hypothetical, Professor Dershowitz segues to the realm of reality: "If torture is, in fact, being used and/or would, in fact, be used in an actual ticking bomb terrorist case, would it be normatively better or worse to have such torture regulated by some kind of warrant?" Such a warrant, he tells us, would authorize interrogators to shove steel needles under Arab fingernails. Dershowitz assumes that his putative torture warrants "would reduce the incidence of abuses," since high officials, operating on the record, would never authorize "methods of the kind shown in the Abu Ghraib photographs."

With torture now a key weapon in the war on terror, the time has come to interrogate the logic of the ticking time bomb with a six-point critique. For this scenario embodies our deepest fears and makes most of us quietly—unwittingly—complicit in the Bush Administration's recourse to torture.

The Scenario Is Improbable

Number one: In the real world, the probability that a terrorist might be captured after concealing a ticking nuclear bomb in Times Square and that his captors would somehow recognize his significance is phenomenally slender. The scenario assumes a highly improbable array of variables that runs something like this:

- First, FBI or CIA agents apprehend a terrorist at the precise moment between timer's first tick and bomb's burst.

- Second, the interrogators somehow have sufficiently detailed foreknowledge of the plot to know they must interrogate this very person and do it right now.

- Third, these same officers, for some unexplained reason, are missing just a few critical details that only this captive can divulge.

- Fourth, the biggest leap of all, these officers with just one shot to get the information that only this captive can divulge are best advised to try torture, as if beating him is the way to ensure his wholehearted cooperation.

Take the case of Zacarias Moussaoui,[3] who sat in a Minneapolis cell in the weeks before 9/11 under desultory investigation as a possible "suicide hijacker" because the FBI did not have precise foreknowledge of Al Qaeda's plot or his possible role. In pressing for a search warrant before 9/11, the bureau's Minneapolis field supervisor even warned Washington he was "trying to keep someone from taking a plane and crashing into the World Trade Center." But FBI headquarters in Washington replied there was no evidence Moussaoui was a terrorist—providing us with yet another reminder of how difficult it is to grasp the significance of even such stunningly accurate insight or intelligence in the absence of foreknowledge.

3. Zacarias Moussaoui was convicted of involvement in the planning of the September 11 attacks.

"After the event," Roberta Wohlstetter wrote in her classic study of that other great U.S. intelligence failure, Pearl Harbor[4] "a signal is always crystal clear; we can now see what disaster it was signaling since the disaster has occurred. But before the event, it is obscure and pregnant with conflicting meanings."

Torture Does Not Work

Number two: This scenario still rests on the critical, utterly unexamined assumption that torture can get useful intelligence quickly from this or any hardened terrorist.

Advocates of the ticking bomb often cite the brutal torture of Abdul Hakim Murad in Manila in 1995, which they say stopped a plot to blow up a dozen trans-Pacific aircraft and kill 4,000 innocent passengers. Except, of course, for the simple fact that Murad's torture did nothing of the sort. As *The Washington Post* has reported, Manila police got all their important information from Murad in the first few minutes when they seized his laptop with the entire bomb plot. All the supposed details gained from the sixty-seven days of incessant beatings, spiced by techniques like cigarettes to the genitals, were, as one Filipino officer testified in a New York court, fabrications fed to Murad by Philippine police.

Even if the terrorist begins to talk under torture, interrogators have a hard time figuring out whether he is telling the truth or not. Testing has found that professional interrogators perform within the 45 to 60 percent range in separating truth from lies—little better than flipping a coin. Thus, as intelligence data moves through three basic stages—acquisition, analysis, and action—the chances that good intelligence will be ignored are high.

4. On December 7, 1941, Japanese war planes bombed the U.S. Naval Base at Pearl Harbor, Hawaii, killing more than 2,400 Americans.

An Interrogator Speaks About Torture

From my experience—and I speak as someone who has personally interrogated many terrorists and elicited important actionable intelligence—I strongly believe that it is a mistake to use what has become known as the "enhanced interrogation techniques." . . .

These techniques, from an operational perspective, are ineffective, slow and unreliable, and as a result harmful to our efforts to defeat al Qaeda. (This is aside from the important additional considerations that they are un-American and harmful to our reputation and cause.). . .

Most of my professional career has been spent investigating, studying, and interrogating terrorists. . . .

In my capacity as a FBI Agent, I investigated and supervised highly sensitive and complex international terrorism cases, including the East Africa bombings the *USS Cole* bombing and the events surrounding the attacks of 9/11. . . .

Ali Soufan, "Testimony of Ali Soufan,"
United States Senate Committee on the Judiciary,
May 13, 2009. http://judiciary.senate.gov.

After fifty years of fighting enemies, communist and terrorist, with torture, we now have sufficient evidence to conclude that torture of the few yields little useful information. As the ancient Roman jurist Ulpian noted 1,800 years ago, when tortured the strong will resist and the weak will say anything to end the pain.

History is replete with examples of the strong who resisted even the most savage tortures. After the July 20, 1944, bomb plot against [Nazi dictator Adolf] Hitler, the Gestapo [Nazi

Germany's Secret Police] subjected Fabian von Schlabrendorff to four weeks of torture by metal spikes and beatings so severe he suffered a heart attack. But with a stoicism typical of these conspirators, he broke his silence only to give the Gestapo a few scraps of vague information when he feared involuntarily blurting out serious intelligence.

Then there are the weak. Ibn al-Shaykh al-Libi, a senior Al Qaeda leader, under torture told his captors that Iraq trained Al Qaeda in chemical and biological weapons. This raises the possibility that he, like Murad, had been tortured into giving fabricated intelligence. [U.S. Secretary of State] Colin Powell relied on this false information in his now-disavowed speech to the United Nations [on February 5, 2003] before the Iraq War.

As Yale legal historian John Langbein puts it, "History's most important lesson is that it has not been possible to make coercion compatible with truth."

Empathic Interrogation

Proponents of torture present a false choice between tortured intelligence and no intelligence at all. There is, in fact, a well-established American alternative to torture that we might call empathetic interrogation. U.S. Marines first used this technique during World War II to extract accurate intelligence from fanatical Japanese captives on Saipan and Tinian[5] within forty-eight hours of landing, and the FBI has practiced it with great success in the decades since. After the East Africa bombings of U.S. embassies [in 1998] the bureau employed this method to gain some of our best intelligence on Al Qaeda and win U.S. court convictions of all of the accused.

One of the bureau agents who worked on that case, Dan Coleman, has since been appalled by the CIA's coercive methods after 9/11. "Have any of these guys ever tried to talk to

---

5. Saipan and Tinian are part of the Northern Marianas Islands in the Pacific. After being held by the Japanese, they were captured by the United States in 1944.

anyone who's been deprived of his clothes?" Coleman asked. "He's going to be ashamed and humiliated and cold. He'll tell you anything you want to hear to get his clothes back. There's no value in it." By contrast, FBI reliance on due process and empathy proved effective in terror cases by building rapport with detainees.

Bush's example of Zubaydah actually supports Coleman's point. FBI agents say they were getting more out of him before the CIA came in with gloves off.

"Brutalization doesn't work," Coleman concluded from his years in FBI counterterrorism. "We know that. Besides, you lose your soul."

A Slippery Slope

Number three: Once we agree to torture the one terrorist with his hypothetical ticking bomb, then we admit a possibility, even an imperative, for torturing hundreds who might have ticking bombs or thousands who just might have some knowledge about those bombs. "You can't know whether a person knows where the bomb is," explains Georgetown University Law Professor David Cole, "or even if they're telling the truth. Because of this, you end up going down a slippery slope and sanctioning torture in general."

Most of those rounded up by military sweeps in Iraq and Afghanistan for imprisonment at Abu Ghraib and Guantánamo had nothing to do with terrorism. A recent analysis of the Pentagon listing of Guantánamo's 517 detainees reveals that 86 percent were arrested not by U.S. forces but by Northern Alliance[6] and Pakistani warlords eager to collect a $5,000 bounty for every "terrorist" captured.

Ironically, though, torture of the many can produce results, albeit at a surprisingly high political price.

The CIA tortured tens of thousands in Vietnam and the French tortured hundreds of thousands in Algeria. During the

6. The Northern Alliance is an Afghani military-political organization.

Battle of Algiers in 1957, French soldiers arrested 30 percent to 40 percent of all males in the city's Casbah and subjected most of these to what one French officer called "beatings, electric shocks, and, in particular, water torture, which was always the most dangerous technique for the prisoner." Though many resisted to the point of death, mass torture gained sufficient intelligence to break the rebel underground. The CIA's Phoenix program no doubt damaged the Viet Cong's communist infrastructure by torture-interrogation of countless South Vietnamese civilians.

So the choices are clear. Major success from limited, surgical torture is a fable, a fiction. But mass torture of thousands of suspects, some guilty, most innocent, can produce some useful intelligence.

The Cost Is Too High

Number four: Useful intelligence perhaps, but at what cost? The price of torture is unacceptably high because it disgraces and then undermines the country that countenances it. For the French in Algeria, for the Americans in Vietnam, and now for the Americans in Iraq, the costs have been astronomical and have outweighed any gains gathered by torture.

Official sources are nearly unanimous that the yield from the massive Phoenix program, with more than forty prisons across South Vietnam systematically torturing thousands of suspected communists, was surprisingly low. One Pentagon contract study found that, in 1970–71, only 3 percent of the Viet Cong "killed, captured, or rallied were full or probationary Party members above the district level." Not surprisingly, such a brutal pacification effort failed either to crush the Viet Cong or win the support of Vietnamese villagers, contributing to the ultimate U.S. defeat in the Vietnam War.

Similarly, the French army won the Battle of Algiers but soon lost the war for Algeria, in part because their systematic torture delegitimated the larger war effort in the eyes of most

Algerians and many French. "You might say that the Battle of Algiers was won through the use of torture," observed British journalist Sir Alistair Horne, "but that the war, the Algerian war, was lost."

Even the comparatively limited torture at Abu Ghraib[7] has done incalculable damage to America's international prestige.

In short, the intelligence gains are soon overwhelmed by political costs as friends and enemies recoil in revulsion at such calculated savagery.

Indeed, the U.S. Army's current field manual, *FM: Intelligence Interrogation 34–52*, contains an implicit warning about these high political costs: "Revelation of use of torture by U.S. personnel," it warns, "will bring discredit upon the U.S. and its armed forces while undermining domestic and international support for the war effort."

Paranoia Produces Torture

Number five: These dismal conclusions lead to a last, uncomfortable question: If torture produces limited gains at such high political cost, why does any rational American leader condone interrogation practices "tantamount to torture"?

One answer to this question seems to lie with a prescient CIA Cold War observation about Soviet leaders in times of stress. "When feelings of insecurity develop within those holding power," reads an agency analysis of Kremlin leadership applicable to the post-9/11 White House, "they become increasingly suspicious and put great pressures upon the secret police to obtain arrests and confessions. At such times, police officials are inclined to condone anything which produces a speedy 'confession,' and brutality may become widespread." In sum, the powerful often turn to torture in times of crisis, not because it works but because it salves their fears and insecurities with the psychic balm of empowerment.

---

7. At Abu Ghraib prison in Iraq, American personnel tortured, raped, and murdered prisoners; the abuses became public in 2004, a year after the U.S. invasion.

As we slide down the slippery slope to torture in general, we should also realize that there is a chasm at the bottom called extrajudicial execution. With the agency's multinational gulag full of dozens, even hundreds, of detainees of dwindling utility, CIA agents, active and retired, have been vocal in their complaints about the costs and inconvenience of limitless, even lifetime, incarceration for these tortured terrorists. The ideal solution to this conundrum from an agency perspective is pump and dump, as in Vietnam—pump the terrorists for information, and then dump the bodies. After all, the systematic French torture of thousands from the Casbah of Algiers in 1957 also entailed more than 3,000 "summary executions" as "an inseparable part" of this campaign, largely, as one French general put it, to ensure that "the machine of justice" not be "clogged with cases." For similar reasons, the CIA's Phoenix program [during the Vietnam War] produced, by the agency's own count, over 20,000 extrajudicial killings.

Number six: The use of torture to stop ticking bombs leads ultimately to a cruel choice—either legalize this brutality, à la Dershowitz and Bush, or accept that the logical corollary to state-sanctioned torture is state-sponsored murder, à la Vietnam.

> *"Anyone who felt the way I felt after 9/11 has to reckon with the fact that what was done in our name was, in some sense, done for us . . . with our blessing."*

Executive Decisions About Torture Are Morally Ambiguous

Ross Douthat

Ross Douthat is a conservative thinker and writer who has contributed to The Atlantic *and* The New York Times, *among other publications. In the following viewpoint, he says he cannot fully condemn the George W. Bush Administration for its use of torture. He argues that after the terrorist attacks of September 11, 2001, Americans such as himself expected the government to use strong measures. In hindsight, using torture turned out to be a very bad decision, Douthat argues, but since he did not himself see the consequences, he feels sympathy for an administration that was trying, in difficult circumstances, to protect American lives.*

Ross Douthat, "Thinking About Torture," *The Atlantic*, December 16, 2008. Reproduced by permission of the author.

As you read, consider the following questions:

1. According to Ross Douthat, what sort of treatment constitutes "torture-lite"?

2. According to Douthat, what factions have presented the most compelling and intellectually consistent condemnations of the Bush Administration torture policy?

3. Douthat says the bombing of Hiroshima and Nagasaki is difficult to justify within what framework?

I haven't written anything substantial, ever, about America's treatment of detainees in the War on Terror. There are good reasons for this, and bad ones. Or maybe there's only one reason, and it's probably a bad one—a desire to avoid taking on a fraught and desperately importantly subject without feeling extremely confident about my own views on the subject.

More Muddiness Needed

I keep waiting, I think, for somebody else to write a piece about the subject that eloquently captures my own inarticulate mix of anger, uncertainty and guilt about the [George W.] Bush Administration's interrogation policy, so that I can just point to their argument and say go read *that*. But so far as I know, nobody has. There's been straightforward outrage, obviously, from many quarters, and then there's been a lot of evasion—especially on the Right, where occasional defenses of torture in extreme scenarios have coexisted with a remarkable silence about the broad writ the Bush Administration seems to have extended to physically abusive interrogation, and the human costs thereof. But to my knowledge, nobody's written something that captures the sheer *muddiness* that surrounds my own thinking (such as it is) on the issue.

That muddiness may reflect moral and/or intellectual confusion on my part, since the grounds for straightforward outrage are pretty obvious. There's a great deal of political tendentiousness woven into Jane Mayer's *The Dark Side*,[1] for instance, but it's very difficult to come away from her reportage unpersuaded that this Administration's counterterrorism policies exposed significant numbers of people—many guilty, but some innocent—to forms of detention and interrogation that we would almost certainly describe as torture if they were carried out by a lawless or dictatorial regime. For a less vivid but also somewhat less partisan analysis that reaches the same conclusion, you can read the executive summary of the just-released Levin-McCain report.[2] (And of course both Mayer's book and the Armed Services Committee report are just the latest in a line of similar findings, by reporters and government investigations alike.)

Now it's true that a great deal of what seems to have been done to detainees arguably falls into the category of what Mark Bowden, in his post-9/11 [after the September 11, 2001, terrorist attacks on America] *Atlantic* essay on "The Dark Art of Interrogation," called "torture lite": It's been mostly "stress positions," extreme temperatures, and "smacky-face," not thumbscrews and branding irons. But it's also clear now, in a way that it wasn't when these things were still theoretical to most Americans, that the torture/torture lite distinction gets pretty blurry pretty quickly in practice. It's clear from the deaths suffered in American custody. It's clear from the testimony that Mayer puts together in her book. And it's clear from the outraged response, among conservatives and liberals alike, to the photographs from Abu Ghraib,[3] which were almost all of practices closer to "torture-lite" than outright torture but which met, justly I think, with near-universal condemnation nonetheless. (And while it still may be true that in some sense, the horrors of Abu Ghraib involved individual

1. Jane Mayer's *The Dark Side*, published in 2008, examined the Bush Administration's war on terror.
2. The Levin-McCain report is a report of the Senate Armed Services Committee on the treatment of detainees, released in December 2008.
3. Abu Ghraib was a U.S.-controlled prison in Iraq following the 2003 U.S. invasion. In 2004, evidence was released showing that U.S. guards had tortured prisoners.

bad apples running amok, they clearly weren't running all that *far* amok, since an awful lot [of] the things they photographed themselves doing—maybe not the human pyramids, but the dogs, the hoods, the nudity and so forth—showed up on lists of interrogation techniques approved by the Secretary of Defense [Donald Rumsfeld] himself.)

So as far as the bigger picture goes, then, it seems indisputable that in the name of national security, and with the backing of seemingly dubious interpretations of the laws, this Administration pursued policies that delivered many detainees to physical and mental abuse, and not a few to death. These were wartime measures, yes, but war is not a moral blank check: If you believe that Abu Ghraib constituted a failure of *jus in bello* [the laws of war], then you have to condemn the decisions that led to Abu Ghraib, which means that you have to condemn the President and his Cabinet.

A Difficult Choice

Given this reality, whence my uncertainty about how to think about the issue? Basically, it stems from the following thought: That while the Bush Administration's policies clearly failed a just-war test, they didn't fail it in quite so *new* a way as some of their critics suppose . . . and moreover, had I been in their shoes I might have failed the test as well. On the first point, I actually *have* found an essay that captures my sentiments; it's Wesley Yang's review of *The Dark Side*, in which he writes as follows:

> The polemical energy of Mayer's book comes from her outrage at the violation of these values. In her introduction, she characterises the Bush Administration's conduct in the War on Terror as "a quantum leap beyond earlier blots on the country's history and history," and "a dramatic break with the past." She invokes the judgment of the eminent liberal historian Arthur Schlesinger, Jr., that "no position taken has done more damage to the American reputation in the world—ever."

But Mayer overplays her hand, going on to write that "in fighting to liberate the world from Communism, Fascism and Nazism, and working to ameliorate global ignorance and poverty, America had done more than any nation on earth to abolish torture and other violations of human rights." Here Mayer confuses the fact that America has always supported human rights in principle with the idea that it has always championed them in practice.

The tactics of the New Paradigm, after all, did not have to be invented from whole cloth. After September 11, [Vice President Dick] Cheney turned to the CIA's [Central Intelligence Agency] archives in search of examples that had worked in the past. "He was particularly impressed," Mayer writes, "with the Vietnam War-era Phoenix Program."

"Critics, including military historians, have described it as a programme of state-sanctioned torture and murder. A Pentagon contract study later found that 97 per cent of the Viet Cong it targeted were of negligible importance. But as of September 11, inside the CIA, the Phoenix Program served as a model." . . .

America has always remained true to its values—except in the rather numerous instances when it has violated them.

Yang describes this as one of "the genuine paradoxes of power that no nation-state aspiring to global leadership can evade." And indeed, the most compelling and intellectually consistent condemnations of the Bush Administration have come from precisely those factions—on the left, and also the small-r republican right—who believe that the United States should *not* aspire to global leadership, because such aspirations require unacceptable compromises with the bloody realities involved in power politics and empire.

What Should Be Allowed?

For those of us, though, who persist in the belief that some sort of American global leadership is better, for all its inherent problems, than most of the alternatives, Yang's analysis has to

Torture and Abu Ghraib

The abuse of detainees at Abu Ghraib in late 2003 was not simply the result of a few soldiers acting on their own. Interrogation techniques such as stripping detainees of their clothes, placing them in stress positions, and using military working dogs to intimidate them appeared in Iraq only after they had been approved for use in Afghanistan and at GTMO [Guantanamo Bay Naval Base in Cuba]. Secretary of Defense Donald Rumsfeld's December 2, 2002, authorization of aggressive interrogation techniques and subsequent interrogation policies and plans approved by senior military and civilian officials conveyed the message that physical pressures and degradation were appropriate treatment for detainees in U.S. military custody. What followed was an erosion in standards dictating that detainees be treated humanely.

Senate Armed Services Committee Inquiry
into the Treatment of Detainees in U.S. Custody,
December 11, 2008. http://levin.senate.gov.

be reckoned with in ways that go beyond simply describing Gitmo [Guantanamo Bay Naval Base in Cuba], Abu Ghraib, and the CIA "black sites" as unique affronts to American values. These and other Bush-era sins have to be considered in the context of previous moral compromises that we've found a way to live with.

For instance: The use of the atomic bomb. I think it's very, very difficult to justify Harry Truman's decision to bomb Hiroshima and Nagasaki in any kind of plausible just-war framework,[4] and if that's the case then the nuclear destruction of

4. Just-war is a Christian ethical tradition that deals with warfare.

two Japanese cities—and indeed, the tactics employed in our bombing campaigns against Germany and Japan more broadly—represents a "war crime" that makes Abu Ghraib look like a trip to Pleasure Island. (And this obviously has implications for the justice of our entire Cold War nuclear posture as well.) But in so thinking, I also have to agree with [World War II historian] Richard Frank's argument that "it is hard to imagine anyone who could have been president at the time (a spectrum that includes FDR [Franklin D. Roosevelt], Henry Wallace, William O. Douglas, Harry Truman, and Thomas Dewey) failing to authorize use of the atomic bombs"—in no small part because I find it hard to imagine *myself* being in Truman's shoes and deciding the matter differently, my beliefs about just-war principle notwithstanding.

The same difficulty obtains where certain forms of torture are concerned. If I find it hard to condemn Harry Truman for incinerating tens of thousands of Japanese civilians, even though I think his decision probably violated the moral framework that should govern the conduct of war, I *certainly* find it hard to condemn the waterboarding[5] of, say, a Khalid Sheikh Muhammed[6] in the aftermath of an event like 9/11, and with more such attacks presumably in the planning stages. I disagree with [syndicated columnist and political commentator] Charles Krauthammer, who has called torture in such extreme circumstances a "moral duty"; rather, I would describe it as a kind of immorality that we cannot expect those charged with the public's safety to always and everywhere refrain from. (Perhaps this means, as some have suggested, that we should ban torture, but issue retroactive pardons to an interrogator who crosses the line when confronted with extreme circumstances and high-value targets. But I suspect that this "maybe you'll get retroactive immunity, wink wink" approach prob-

5. Waterboarding is a form of torture in which water is poured into a victim's airway, resulting in controlled drowning.
6. Khalid Sheikh Muhammed is a terrorist who was involved in the planning of the 9/11 attacks.

ably places too great a burden on the individual interrogator, and that ultimately some kind of mechanism is required whereby the use of extreme measures in extreme circumstances is brought within the law.)

Yet of course the waterboarding of al Qaeda's high command, despite the controversy it's generated, is not in fact the biggest moral problem posed by the Bush Administration's approach to torture and interrogation. The biggest problem is the sheer scope of the physical abuse that was endorsed from on high—the way it was routinized, extended to an ever-larger pool of detainees, and delegated ever-further down the chain of command. Here I'm more comfortable saying straightforwardly that *this should never have been allowed*—that it should be considered impermissible as well as immoral, and that it should involve disgrace for those responsible, the Cheneys and Rumsfelds as well as the people who actually implemented the techniques that the Vice President's office promoted and the Secretary of Defense signed off on.[7]

But here, too, I have uncertainty, mixed together with guilt, about how strongly to condemn those involved—because in a sense I know that what they were doing was what I wanted them to do.

Doing What We Wanted

Oh, not in every particular: As was often the case with the Bush Administration, I didn't envision many of the stupidities involved (reverse-engineering interrogation from training exercises designed to prepare for ChiCom brainwashing? really?); or the way that the debates over torture would intersect with controversies over executive power, the design of military tribunals, and so forth; or the precise scale and scope that any "torture-lite" program would take on. But I certainly remember how I felt about interrogation in the aftermath of 9/11: I

---

7. Vice President Dick Cheney and Secretary of Defense Donald Rumsfeld both supported enhanced interrogation measures or torture.

felt that we were *all* suddenly in a ticking-bomb scenario, that the gloves have to come off, and that all kinds of things needed to be on the table. When Dick Cheney said that we have to work on "the dark side" in the post-9/11 environment, I thought that he was only stating the obvious. When Cofer Black, the CIA man who's depicted, perhaps unfairly, as a blundering fool in Mayer's account, appeared in accounts of Bush's late-2001 cabinet meetings as the guy who said of Al Qaeda, "when we're through with them they will have flies walking across their eyeballs," my instinctive reaction was *hell yeah*. And when Bowden walked *Atlantic* readers through the debate over torture-lite, I knew whose side I was on. Read it for yourself:

> The word "torture" comes from the Latin verb *torquere*, "to twist." *Webster's New World Dictionary* offers the following primary definition: "The inflicting of severe pain to force information and confession, get revenge, etc." Note the adjective "severe," which summons up images of the rack, thumbscrews, gouges, branding irons, burning pits, impaling devices, electric shock, and all the other devilish tools devised by human beings to mutilate and inflict pain on others. All manner of innovative cruelty is still commonplace, particularly in Central and South America, Africa, and the Middle East. . . .
>
> Then there are methods that, some people argue, fall short of torture. Called "torture lite," these include sleep deprivation, exposure to heat or cold, the use of drugs to cause confusion, rough treatment (slapping, shoving, or shaking), forcing a prisoner to stand for days at a time or to sit in uncomfortable positions, and playing on his fears for himself and his family. Although excruciating for the victim, these tactics generally leave no permanent marks and do no lasting physical harm.
>
> The Geneva Convention makes no distinction: it bans any mistreatment of prisoners. But some nations that are other-

wise committed to ending brutality have employed torture lite under what they feel are justifiable circumstances. . . . As these interrogators see it, the well-being of the captive must be weighed against the lives that might be saved by forcing him to talk. A method that produces life-saving information without doing lasting harm to anyone is not just preferable; it appears to be morally sound.

Reading Mayer's book, the recent Senate report, and other sources, it seems clear that this was roughly the logic that motivated much of what was authorized in CIA prisons, in Gitmo, and eventually in a suicide-bomber-raddled Iraq—a logic that convinced figures like Rumsfeld and George Bush that they were stopping short of torture (think of Rumsfeld's dismissive margin comment, as he authorized long-term standing, that *he* stood for 8–10 hours a day, so why shouldn't prisoners?) even as the the practices they authorized led inexorably to abuse, violence and even death.

Understandable Mistakes

Some of the most passionate torture opponents have stated that they never, ever imagined that the Bush Administration would even consider authorizing the sort of interrogation techniques described above, to say nothing of more extreme measures like waterboarding. I was not so innocent, or perhaps I should say I was more so: If you had listed, in the aftermath of 9/11, most of the things that have been done to prisoners by representatives of the U.S. government, I would have said that *of course* I expected the Bush Administration to authorize "stress positions," or "slapping, shoving and shaking," or the use of heat and cold to elicit information. After all, there was a war on! I just had no idea—until the pictures came out of Abu Ghraib, and really until I started reading detailed accounts of how detainees were being treated—what these methods could mean in practice, and especially as practiced on a global scale. A term like "stress positions" sounds like one thing when it's sitting, bloodless, on a page; it sounds like something else when somebody dies from it. . . .

With great power comes the responsibility to exercise better judgment than, say, my twenty-three-year-old, pro-torture-lite self. But with great power comes a lot of pressures as well, starting with great fear: The fear that through *inaction* you'll be responsible for the deaths of thousands or even millions of the Americans whose lives you were personally charged to protect. This fear ran wild [in] the post-9/11 Bush Administration, with often-appalling consequences, but it wasn't an irrational fear—not then, and [not] now. It doesn't excuse what was done by our government, and in our name, in prisons and detention cells around the world. But anyone who felt the way I felt after 9/11 has to reckon with the fact that what was done in our name was, in some sense, done for us—not with our knowledge, exactly, but arguably with our blessing. I didn't get what I wanted from this administration, but I think you could say with some justification that I got what I asked for. And that awareness undergirds—to return to where I began this rambling [viewpoint]—the mix of anger, uncertainty and guilt that I bring to the current debate over what the Bush Administration has done and failed to do, and how its members should be judged.

> *"One cannot coherently sanction or even acquiesce to serious government law-breaking and then feign outrage over illegal torture and other war crimes."*

Executive Use of Torture Shows an Unambiguous Contempt for the Law

Glenn Greenwald

Glenn Greenwald is a lawyer and a columnist for Salon.com. *In the following viewpoint, he argues that the use of torture is part of a broader breakdown of the rule of law. He contends that the George W. Bush administration and its supporters believe that there are no legal limits on presidential power in fighting terrorism. He argues that those who claim to be morally conflicted about torture or who feel the administration should not be held accountable for its actions undermine the government-by-law that is the basis of a civilized society.*

Glenn Greenwald, "Torture and the Rule of Law," Salon.com, July 12, 2008. This article first appeared in Salon.com at http://www.salon.com. An online version remains in the Salon archives. Reprinted with permission.

As you read, consider the following questions:

1. According to Glenn Greenwald, what is the well-intentioned debate Andrew Sullivan is having with himself and his readers?

2. What does Greenwald give as examples of issues that are not composed of two reasonable sides?

3. What does Greenwald say is the most destructive aspect of the Foreign Intelligence Surveillance Act (FISA) law?

The New Yorker's Jane Mayer, one of the country's handful of truly excellent investigative journalists over the last seven years [2001–2008], has written a new book—*The Dark Side: The Inside Story of How the War on Terror Turned into a War on American Ideals*—which reveals several extraordinary (though unsurprising) facts regarding America's torture regime. According to the *New York Times* [*NYT*] and *Washington Post*, both of which received an advanced copy, Mayer's book reports the following:

Torture and Mistaken Arrest

- "Red Cross investigators concluded last year [2007] in a secret report that the Central Intelligence Agency's [CIA] interrogation methods for high-level al-Qaeda prisoners *constituted torture and could make the [George W.] Bush administration officials who approved them guilty of war crimes.*"

- "A CIA analyst warned the Bush administration in 2002 that *up to a third of the detainees at Guantanamo Bay may have been imprisoned by mistake,* but House officials ignored the finding and insisted that all were 'enemy combatants' subject to indefinite incarceration."

- "[A] top aide to Vice President [Dick] Cheney shrugged off the report and squashed proposals for a quick review of the detainees' cases. . . .

- 'There will be no review,' the book quotes Cheney staff director David Addington as saying. 'The president has determined that they are *ALL* enemy combatants. We are not going to revisit it.'"

- "[T]he [CIA] analyst estimated that a full third of the camp's detainees were there by mistake. When told of those findings, the top military commander at Guantanamo at the time, Major Gen. Michael Dunlavey, not only agreed with the assessment but suggested that *an even higher percentage of detentions—up to half—were in error*. Later, an academic study by Seton Hall University Law School concluded that 55 percent of detainees had never engaged in hostile acts against the United States, and only 8 percent had any association with al-Qaeda."

- [T]he International Committee of the Red Cross declared in the report, given to the CIA last year, that the methods used on Abu Zubaydah, the first major al-Qaeda figure the United States captured, *were 'categorically' torture, which is illegal under both American and international law.*

- "[T]he Red Cross document 'warned that the abuse constituted war crimes, placing the highest officials in the U.S. government in jeopardy of being prosecuted.'"

No Rule of Law

This is what a country becomes when it decides that it will not live under the rule of law, when it communicates to its political leaders that they are free to do whatever they want—including breaking our laws—and there will be no consequences. There are two choices and only two choices for every country—live under the rule of law or live under the ride of men. We've collectively decided that our most powerful political leaders are not bound by our laws—that when they break the law, there will be no consequences. We've thus become a country which lives under the proverbial "rule of men"—that is literally true, with no hyperbole needed—and Mayer's revelations are nothing more than the inevitable by-product of that choice.

That's why this ongoing, well-intentioned debate that Andrew Sullivan[1] is having with himself and his readers over whether "torture is worse than illegal, warrantless eavesdropping" is so misplaced, and it's also why those who are dismissing as "an overblown distraction" the anger generated by last week's Congressional protection of surveillance lawbreakers are so deeply misguided.[2] Things like "torture" and "illegal eavesdropping" can't be compared as though they're separate, competing policies. They are rooted in the same framework of lawlessness. The same rationale that justifies one is what justifies the other. Endorsing one is to endorse all of it.

In fact, none of the scandals of radicalism and criminality which we've learned about over the last seven years—including the creation of this illegal torture regime—can be viewed in isolation. They're all by-products of the country that we've become in the post-9/11 era [after the terrorist attacks of September 11, 2001], *primarily* as a result of our collective decision to exempt our Government leaders from the rule of law; to acquiesce to the manipulative claim that we can only be Safe if we allow our Leaders to be free from consequences when they commit crimes; and to demonize advocates of the rule of law as—to use Larry Lessig's[3] mindless, reactionary clichés—shrill, Leftist "hysterics" who need to "get off [their] high horse(s)".

1. Andrew Sullivan is a blogger who has spoken out frequently against torture.
2. The George W. Bush Administration instituted a program that allowed the National Security Agency (NSA) to tap phones without warrants. Congress in 2008 voted to protect from prosecution the telephone companies that had gone along with the administration.
3. Larry Lessig is a professor of law at Stanford University.

That is the mentality that has allowed the Bush administration to engage in this profound assault on our national character, to violate our laws at will. Our political and media elite have acquiesced to all of this when they weren't cheering it all on. Those who object to it, who argue that these abuses of political power are dangerous in the extreme and that we cannot tolerate deliberate government lawbreaking, are dismissed as shrill Leftist hysterics.

All the way back in May 2006—just months after the *NYT* revealed the illegal NSA spying program—I wrote in my first book, *How Would a Patriot Act*, the following about the NSA eavesdropping scandal:

> This is not about eavesdropping. This is about whether we are a nation of laws. . . . The heart of the matter is that the President broke the law, repeatedly and deliberately, no matter what his rationale for doing so was. . . .

> The National Security Agency eavesdropping scandal is not an isolated act of lawbreaking. It is an outgrowth of an ideology of lawlessness that has been adopted by the Bush administration as its governing doctrine. Others include the incarceration in military prisons of U.S. citizens who were not charged with any crime or even allowed access to a lawyer, the use of legally prohibited torture techniques, and the establishment of a military detention center in Guantanamo Bay, a no-man's-land that the administration claims is beyond the reach of U.S. law. In the media and the public mind, these issues have been seen in isolation, as though they are unconnected.

> In fact, all of these controversial actions can be traced to a single cause, a shared root. They are grounded in, and are the by-product of, an unprecedented and truly radical theory of presidential power that, at its core, maintains that the president's power is literally unlimited and absolute in matters relating to terrorism or national security. . . .

What we have in our federal government are not individual acts of lawbreaking or isolated scandals of illegality, but instead a culture and an ideology of lawlessness.

The President Can Do Anything

But those who argued such things were The Shrill Leftists, The Crazed Civil-Liberties Extremists, the Hysterics. And they still are. By contrast, Serious People understood—and still understand—that our leaders made complex and weighty decisions for our own Good and that terms like "lawbreaking" and "war crimes" and "prosecutions" have no place in respectable American political circles. Hence, our political leaders operate in a climate where they know they can do anything—anything at all, including flagrantly breaking our most serious laws—and they will be defended, or at least have their behavior mitigated, by a virtually unanimous political and media establishment. The hand-wringing over Mayer's latest revelations will be led by the very people who are responsible for what has taken place—responsible because they decided that rampant, deliberate lawbreaking by our Government officials was nothing to get worked up over.

There are many political disputes—probably most—composed of two or more reasonable sides. Whether the U.S. Government has committed war crimes by torturing detainees—conduct that is illegal under domestic law and international treaties which are binding law in this country—isn't an example of a reasonable, two-sided political dispute. Nor is the issue of whether the U.S. Government and the telecom industry engaged in illegal acts for years by spying on Americans without warrants. Nor is the question of whether we should allow Government officials to break our laws at will by claiming that doing so is necessary to keep us Safe.

There just aren't two sides to those matters. That's what the International Red Cross means when it says that what we did to Guantanamo detainees was "categorically torture." It's what the only federal judges to adjudicate the question—all three—have concluded when they found that the President clearly broke our laws with no valid excuses by spying on our communications for years with no warrants. It's why the Bush administration has sought—and repeatedly received—immunity and amnesty for the people who have implemented these policies. It's because these actions are clearly illegal—criminal—and we all know that.

And that's true no matter how many Bush-loyal DOJ [Department of Justice] lawyers justify the behavior, no matter how many right-wing lawyers go on TV to defend the Government's conduct, no matter how many Brookings[4] "scholars" go to *The New Republic* in order flamboyantly to boast how deeply complex these matters are and how only Super-Experts (like themselves) can grapple with the fascinating intellectual puzzles they pose. Displaying cognitive angst and/or above-it-all indifference in the face of unambiguously illegal and morally reprehensible government conduct isn't a sign of intellectual sophistication or political Seriousness. It's exactly the opposite. It's the hallmark of complicity with it.

Law Professor Jonathan Turley, on MSNBC last night [July 2008] discussing Mayer's revelation, put it this way:

[The International Red Cross (IRC)] is the world's preeminent institution on the conditions and treatment of prisoners and specifically what constitutes torture. And the important thing here is they're saying *it's not a close question*, that as many of us, and there are many, many of us who have argued for years that this is *clearly, unmistakably a torture program*; the Red Cross is saying same.

The problem for the Bush administration is they perfected plausible deniability techniques. They bring out one or two people that are willing to debate on cable shows whether water-boarding is torture. And it leaves the impression that

---

4. The Brookings Institution is a nonpartisan think tank.

it's a close question. *It's just like the domestic surveillance program that the a federal court just a week ago also said was not a close question. These are illegal acts. These are crimes.* And there weren't questions before and there's not questions now as to the illegality. . . .

I never thought I would say this, but I think it might, in fact, be time for the United States to be held internationally to a tribunal. I never thought, in my lifetime, that I would say that, that we have become like Serbia, where an international tribunal has to come to force us to apply the rule of law. *I never imagined that a Congress, a Democratic-led Congress would refuse to take actions, even with the preeminent institution of the Red Cross saying, this is clearly torture and torture is a a war crime. They are still refusing to take meaningful action.*

So, we've come to this ignoble moment where we could be forced into a tribunal and forced to face *the rule of law that we've refused to apply to ourselves.*

There Must Be Accountability

That's the inevitable outcome when a country's political establishment decrees itself exempt from the rule of law. If the rule of law doesn't constrain the actions of government officials, then nothing will. Continuous revelations of serious government lawbreaking have led not to investigations or punishment but to retroactive immunity and concealment of the crimes. Judicial findings of illegal government behavior have led to Congressional action to protect the lawbreakers. The Detainee Treatment Act. The Military Commissions Act. The Protect America Act. The FISA [Foreign Intelligence Surveillance Act] Amendments Act.[5] They're all rooted in the same premise: that our highest government leaders have the power to ignore our laws with impunity, and when they're caught, they should be immunized and protected, not punished.

5. All of these are acts of Congress that attempted to expand executive powers or to grant immunity to those who had committed potentially illegal acts.

When our political and media elite aren't defending the Bush administration's lawbreaking, they're dismissing its importance. [Pundit] David Broder believes that government crimes are mere "policy disputes" that shouldn't be punished. And here's "liberal" pundit Tim Rutten of *The Los Angeles Times*, acknowledging that our highest political officials ordered illegal torture, but then invoking the very common—and indescribably destructive—mentality of most of our Good Establishment Liberals to insist that they should not be held legally accountable:

> It's true that there are a handful of European rights activists and *people on the lacy left fringe of American politics who would dearly like to see such trials*, but actually pursuing them would be a profound—even tragic—mistake. Our political system works as smoothly as it does, in part, because *we've never criminalized differences over policy*. Since [President] Andrew Jackson's time, our electoral victors celebrate by throwing the losers out of work—not into jail cells. . . .

That warped mentality—as much as the most lawless elements of the Bush administration—is what is responsible for the destruction of our fundamental national character over the last seven years. "Laws" and "crimes" are only for the common people and for other countries. We're too magisterial a country, our political leaders are too Important and too Good, to subject them to punishment when they break our laws. That's the mentality that has created the climate of Lawlessness that defines who we are.

Yes, I'm well aware that the U.S, like all countries, was deeply imperfect prior to 9/11, and that many of the systematic excesses of the Bush era have their genesis prior to 2001. The difference (a critical one) is that what had been acts of lawbreaking and violations of our national values have become the norm—consistent with, rather than violative of, our express values and policies. As Mayer writes in her book:

For the first time in its history, the United States sanctioned government officials to physically and psychologically torment U.S.-held captives, making torture the official law of the land in all but name.

The enactment of the new FISA bill last week[6] [July 10, 2008] was destructive for many reasons, including the fact that it legalized a regime of warrantless eavesdropping that is certain to be abused. But the *far more destructive aspect of the new law* is that it was just the latest example—albeit the most flagrant—of our political class abolishing the rule of law in this country.

It will never stop being jarring that Pulitzer-Prize-winning revelations from the *New York Times* that the President and the telecom industry were committing felonies years culminated in the full-scale protection of the lawbreakers and retroactive legalization of the criminality by the "opposition party" which controls the Congress.

One cannot coherently sanction or even acquiesce to serious government lawbreaking and then feign outrage over illegal torture and other war crimes. The sanctioning of government illegality is precisely what leads to abuses like the American torture regime. Those who have spent the last seven years scoffing at Unserious, Hysterical objections to Bush lawlessness are the very people who have created this climate that they will now pretend to find so upsetting. The "rule of law" isn't some left-wing dogma that is the province of Leftist radicals and hysterics. It's the cornerstone of every civilized and free society, and Jane Mayer's new book is but the latest piece of evidence to prove that.

---

6. The FISA bill was the bill that immunized telecom companies from prosecution.

| "Coercion ... is used by good guys and bad guys alike. ... The morality of violence depends in large part on the motives behind it."

Torture Is Sometimes Justified

Jonah Goldberg

Jonah Goldberg is a conservative syndicated columnist and the author of Liberal Fascism. *In the following viewpoint, he argues that moderate coercive methods, like striking a suspect, are different from full-scale torture. He also maintains that torturing someone to save innocent lives is different from torturing out of sadism. As evidence that his view is widely shared, he points to television and movies, in which good guys often resort to coercion. Because many audiences enjoy such entertainment, Goldberg concludes that there is public support for some torture, and that the issue of whether torture is justified is complicated rather than self-evident.*

As you read, consider the following questions:

1. What sort of torture does Jonah Goldberg say everyone is against except in ticking-time bomb scenarios?

Jonah Goldberg, "Harrison Ford & The Ticking Time Bomb," *National Review Online*, December 2005. Reproduced by permission of Tribune Media Services.

2. What movies and television shows does Goldberg say treat torture in a positive light?

3. What percentage of Americans believe torture can be justified in some cases, according to an Associated Press-Ipsos poll?

The answer isn't as obvious as you think. Sure, as a political force, Hollywood is against torture, which ranks somewhere in the parade of horribles ahead of SUV ownership and perhaps even voting Republican. No doubt Barbra Streisand and Alec Baldwin[1] have delivered many a dinner-table stemwinder against the [George W.] Bush administration's defense of "coercive measures" in extreme circumstances.

And to be fair, the Hollywood crowd isn't alone. Back here in Washington, the issue of torture has largely united liberals and divided conservatives. One of the main disagreements is what people mean by torture. If you mean hot pokers in unwelcome places, pretty much everyone is against it, save perhaps in the famous "ticking-time bomb" scenario.[2]

Is Torture Always Wrong?

But the meatier part of the argument is in the more nuanced area of "coercive measures," "stress positions," and what one unnamed official once described to the *Wall Street Journal* as "a little bit of smacky-face." Some, such as Republican Senators John McCain and Lindsey Graham want even that stuff banned (but acknowledge that if it comes to a ticking-time bomb situation, well, "you do what you have to do," as McCain put it).

Others go even further than that. Naturally, human-rights groups are appalled by the suggestion that harsh treatment is

1. Barbra Streisand and Alec Baldwin are both performers who have been identified with liberal causes.
2. The ticking-time bomb scenario is the argument that torture is justified to obtain information that would help to defuse an imminent, catastrophic threat such as a ticking time bomb.

ever justified. Similarly, blogger Andrew Sullivan[3] dismisses the ticking-time bomb as a "red herring" and argues that "you cannot raise or lower the moral status of mass murderers with respect to torture. The only salient moral status with respect to torture is that the mass murderers are human beings."

In other words, it doesn't matter what the person you are coercing did or why you are coercing them in the first place. Torturing an evil man to save innocent lives is no greater a sin than torturing a noble man in order to snuff out innocent lives, or just for the fun of it. The way Sullivan and those who agree with him see it, torture is torture is torture—and torture is always wrong, even when defined as intimidation and "smacky face." "Not in my name," is their rallying cry, often with the sort of sanctimony and self-righteousness which suggests that those who disagree must admire cruelty.

Hollywood Shows Torture's Complexity

And that's where Hollywood comes in. Politically, Hollywood is fairly two dimensional in its liberalism. But artistically—and to its credit—Hollywood seems to grasp that life can be morally complicated. After all, tactics which qualify as torture for the anti-crowd show up in film and television every day. On *NYPD Blue*, Andy Sipowicz, played by Dennis Franz, smacked around criminals all the time. In *Guarding Tess*, Nicolas Cage shot the toe off a man who wouldn't tell him what he wanted to know, and told him he'd keep shooting piggies until he heard what he wanted.

In *Patriot Games*, Harrison Ford shot a man in the kneecap to get the information he needed in a timely manner. In *Rules of Engagement*, Samuel L. Jackson shot a POW [Prisoner of War] in the head to get another man to talk. In the TV series *24*, the heroes regularly use torture and cruelty to get results. They even mistakenly tortured an innocent woman.

---

3. Andrew Sullivan is a blogger and writer who has often spoken out against torture.

Torture Is a Duty

Breaking the laws of war and abusing civilians are what, to understate the matter vastly, terrorists do for a living. They are entitled, therefore, to nothing. Anyone who blows up a car bomb in a market deserves to spend the rest of his life roasting on a spit over an open fire. But we don't do that because we do not descend to the level of our enemy. . . .

[Then], there is the terrorist with information. Here the issue of torture gets complicated and the easy pieties don't so easily apply. Let's take the textbook case. Ethics 101: A terrorist has planted a nuclear bomb in New York City. It will go off in one hour. A million people will die. You capture the terrorist. He knows where it is. He's not talking.

Question: If you have the slightest belief that hanging this man by his thumbs will get you the information to save a million people, are you permitted to do it?

Now, on most issues regarding torture, I confess tentativeness and uncertainty. But on this issue, there can be no uncertainty: Not only is it permissible to hang this miscreant by his thumbs. It is a moral duty.

Charles Krauthammer,
"The Truth About Torture," The Weekly Standard,
December 5, 2005. www.weeklystandard.com.

And the audience is expected to cheer or at least sympathize with all of it. Now, I know many will say "It's only a movie" or "It's only a TV show." But that will not do. Hollywood plays a role in shaping culture, but it also reflects it. It both affirms and reflects our basic moral sense (which is one reason why it dismays some of us from time to time).

It is hardly imaginable that Hollywood would—or could—make long-running TV shows or successful movies where the protagonist is a soaked-to-the-bone racist. Why? Because audiences would reject the premise and so would filmmakers. But, last I checked, there were no howls of outrage when a racist mayor in *Mississippi Burning* was brutalized and threatened with castration in order to give up information. Heck, the movie was nominated for six Oscars, including best picture and best director.

The issue here is context. Coercion of the sort we're discussing is used by good guys and bad guys alike—in films and in real life. Just as with guns and fistfights, the morality of violence depends in large part on the motives behind it (that's got to be one of the main reasons so many on the left oppose the war: They distrust Bush's motives. Very few of Bush critics are true pacifists).

American audiences—another word for the American public—understand this. A recent poll by AP [Associated Press]-Ipsos shows that some 61 percent of Americans believe torture can be justified in some cases. Interestingly, roughly half of the residents of that self-described "moral superpower" Canada agreed, as did a majority of French citizens and a huge majority of South Koreans.

My guess is that when presented in cinematic form, even larger numbers of people recognize that sometimes good people must do bad things. I'm not suggesting, of course, that the majority is always right. But it should at least suggest to those preening in their righteousness that people of good will can disagree.

> *"To say that the authorities are going to use preventive interrogational torture in catastrophic cases is not the same thing as saying that they should be authorized to do so through . . . legal rules."*

Even Though Torture May Be Justified Sometimes, It Should Always Be Illegal

Oren Gross

Oren Gross is professor of law and director of the Institute for International Legal & Security Studies at the University of Minnesota Law School. In the following viewpoint, he argues that an absolute ban on torture is unrealistic because governments will correctly resort to torture in extreme cases. He also believes, however, that allowing torture has dangerous consequences. Therefore, he argues that torture should be legally banned. In cases where governments do resort to torture because of extreme circumstances, Gross believes they should be held accountable by

Oren Gross, "Are Torture Warrants Warranted? Pragmatic Absolutism and Official Disobedience," *Minnesota Law Review*, vol. 88, 2004, pp. 1511–1526. Reproduced by permission of the author.

the public, which may punish them if their actions seem unwarranted or may pardon them through various mechanisms if their decisions seem justified.

As you read, consider the following questions:

1. Did philosopher Immanuel Kant believe that lying was ever justified?

2. What are the two perspectives from which to approach the question of preventive interrogational torture, according to Oren Gross?

3. According to Gross, what are some legal modes of ratification through which society may pardon torturers?

To deny the use of preventive interrogational torture,[1] even when there is good reason to believe that a massive bomb is ticking away in a crowded mall, is as cold hearted as it is to permit torture in the first place. It is cold hearted because, in true catastrophic cases, the failure to use preventive interrogational torture will result in the death of a great number of innocent people. Upholding the rights of the suspect will negate the rights, including the very fundamental right to life, of innocent victims. I agree with Sissela Bok's [author of *Lying: Moral Choice in Public and Private Life*] observation that "it is a very narrow view of responsibility which does not also take some blame for a disaster one could easily have averted, no matter how much others are also to blame." . . .

Torture Will Be Used

[T]o deny the use of preventive interrogational torture in such cases is also hypocritical: experience tells us that when faced with serious threats to the life of the nation, government— *any* government—will take whatever measures it deems neces-

---

1. Preventive interrogational torture is torture used in questioning a suspect who has information that may save innocent lives.

sary to abate the crisis. In her opinion in *Barzilai v. Government of Israél*, Justice Ben-Porat of the Israeli Supreme Court wrote:

> [W]e, as judges who "dwell among our people," should not harbour any illusions. . . . There simply are cases in which those who are at the helm of the State, and bear responsibility for its survival and security, regard certain deviations from the law for the sake of protecting the security of the State, as an unavoidable necessity.

Ignoring the real-life consequences of catastrophic cases may result in portrayal of the legal system as unrealistic and inadequate. As a result, particular norms, and perhaps the legal system in general, may break down, as the ethos of obedience to law is seriously shaken and challenges emerge with respect to the reasonableness of following these norms. Thus, legal rigidity in the face of severe crises is not merely hypocritical; it may be detrimental to long-term notions of the rule of law. It may also lead to more, rather than less, radical interference with individual rights and liberties. . . .

An uncompromising absolute prohibition on torture sets unrealistic standards that no one can hope to meet when faced with extremely exigent circumstances. Such unrealistic standards would, in fact, either be ineffective or would be perceived as setting double standards. . . .

In fact, even if each of us, as individual moral agents, supported an absolute prohibition on torture, we would still not want those we entrust with keeping us safe from harm to be strictly bound by similar constraints. We want our leaders and public officials to possess the highest moral character, but I do not believe we want them to be brazen Kantians.[2] Recall Kant's celebrated example of an unconditional duty, i.e., the duty to tell the truth. According to Kant, the duty to tell the truth is not suspended even when an assassin (A) asks a person (B)

2. Immanuel Kant was an 18th century German philosopher.

whether he knows the whereabouts of a friend of B, whom A wishes to murder. I agree with Sissela Bok that "[a] world where it is improper even to tell a lie to a murderer pursuing an innocent victim is not a world that many would find safe to inhabit." Very few people would want to have as a friend someone who tells the murderer the truth rather than lie and save her friend. Similarly, few would want a leader who follows Kant's absolutist views to their extreme rather than act to save the lives of innocent civilians. . . .

Thus, there are two perspectives from which to approach the question of preventive interrogational torture: the general policy perspective and the perspective of the catastrophic case. Both perspectives are valuable and relevant. Focusing on one to the exclusion of the other is misguided. However, we must not use the two perspectives simultaneously. Instead, I suggest that the primary perspective ought to be the general one, which, as indicated above, supports an absolute legal ban on torture for a combination of moral and pragmatic considerations. Once this general policy is set in place, we should attend to the real problems that the catastrophic case presents. But can we really examine preventive interrogational torture from both perspectives and still make a coherent, morally and legally defensible argument? I believe we can. . . .

Official Disobedience

When catastrophic cases occur, governments and their agents are likely to do whatever is necessary to neutralize the threat, whether legal or not. Yet, to say that the authorities are going to use preventive interrogational torture in catastrophic cases is not the same thing as saying that they should be authorized to do so through . . . legal rules. It is extremely dangerous to provide for such eventualities and such awesome powers within the framework of the existing legal system primarily because of the enormous risks of contamination and manipulation of that system, and the deleterious message involved in legalizing such actions.

Like everybody else, officials should obey the law, even when they disagree with specific legal commands. However, there may be extreme exigencies where officials may regard strict obedience to legal authority (e.g., an absolute legal ban on torture) irrational or immoral. Absolutists—in this context, those who insist on an unqualified rule of obedience— would resolve the official's dilemma in such cases by finding that her obligation to obey legal authority is undiminished by the extreme exigency. Some consequentialists[3] may argue that the decision whether to obey ought to be made on a case-by-case basis, carefully comparing the relative costs and benefits of each alternative.... [B]oth of these extreme positions are subject to critical challenges....

The proposed model of official disobedience is ... [a] middle ground between the diametrically opposed poles of absolutism and consequentialist conditionalism....

The model of official disobedience calls upon public officials having to deal with catastrophic cases to consider the possibility of acting outside the legal order while openly acknowledging their actions and the extralegal nature of such actions. The officials must assume the risks involved in acting extralegally....

Consider again the possibility of extreme circumstances where officials may regard strict obedience to legal authority as irrational or immoral.... According to the official disobedience model, if an official determines that a particular case necessitates her deviation from a relevant rule, she may choose to depart from the rule. But at the time she acts extralegally, she will not know what the personal consequences of violating the rule are going to be. Not only does the basic rule continue to apply to other situations (that is, it is not canceled or terminated), it is not even overridden (from a legal perspective at least) in the concrete case at hand. Rule departure con-

3. Consequentialists are those who determine the morality of an action based on its likely consequences.

stitutes, under all circumstances and all conditions, a violation of the relevant legal rule. Yet, whether the actor would be punished for her violation remains a separate question. Society, as the imposer of authority, retains the role of making the final determination whether the actor ought to be punished and rebuked, or rewarded and commended for her actions. It should be up to society as a whole, "the people," to decide how to respond . . . to extralegal actions taken by government officials in response to extreme exigencies. The people may decide to hold the actor accountable for the wrongfulness of her actions, or may approve them retrospectively. Thus, even when acting to advance the public good under circumstances of great necessity, officials remain answerable to the public for their extralegal actions. Justice [Robert H.] Jackson was right to suggest [in his dissent in *Korematsu v. United States* (1994)] that "[t]he chief restraint upon those who command the physical forces of the country . . . must be their responsibility to the political judgments of their contemporaries and to the moral judgments of history." At the end of the day, it is those political, moral, and—one may add to the list—legal judgments of the public that serve as the real restraint on public officials.

Society Will Judge

Society may determine that the use of torture in any given case, even when couched in terms of preventing future catastrophes, is abhorrent, unjustified, and inexcusable. In such a case, the acting official may be called to answer for her actions and make legal and political amends. She may, for example, need to resign her position, face criminal charges or civil suits, or be subject to impeachment proceedings. Alternatively, the people may approve the actions and ratify them. Such ratification may be formal or informal, legal as well as social or political. Legal modes of ratification include, for example, the exercise of prosecutorial discretion not to bring criminal

Al Qaeda Threatens Our Values

Al Qaeda does not pose a threat to the United States' (or any of its allies') existence. Its real threat lies in provoking us to employ authoritarian measures that would weaken the fabric of our democracy, discredit the United States internationally, diminish our ability to utilize our soft power and undermine our claim to the moral higher ground in the fight against the terrorists.

In other words, the critical threat is not that the United States would fail to defend itself but that it would do so too well and in the process become less democratic and lose sight of its fundamental values. "Whoever fights monsters," warned Friedrich Nietzsche, "should see to it that in the process he does not become a monster. And if you gaze long enough into an abyss, the abyss will gaze back into you."

Oren Gross, "Commentary: Torture Must Be Investigated," CNNPolitics.com, April 30, 2009. www.cnn.com.

charges against persons accused of using torture, jury nullification where criminal charges are brought, executive pardoning or clemency where criminal proceedings result in conviction, and governmental indemnification of state agents who are found liable for damages to persons who were tortured.

Political and social ratification is also possible. A president who personally authorizes the use of torture may be reelected by a substantial majority in free and democratic elections where the issue of torture constitutes a major part of the pre-election public agenda. Alternatively, she may need to resign her position or face impeachment proceedings. Yale Law Professor Charles Black apparently put the matter to his constitutional law class in the following terms: "[o]nce the torturer extracted the information required . . . he should at once resign to await trial, pardon, and/or a decoration, as the case might be." . . .

The proposed model emphasizes an ethic of responsibility not only on the part of public officials, but also of the general public. Officials will need to acknowledge openly the nature of their actions and attempt to justify both their actions and their undertaking of those actions. This open acknowledgment and engagement in public justificatory exercise is a critical component in the moral and legal choice made by the acting officials. The public then must decide whether to ratify the relevant extralegal actions. During the process of ratification, each member of the public becomes morally and politically responsible for the decision. "[D]ecent men and women, hard-pressed in war, must sometimes do terrible things," writes [political theorist Michael] Walzer, "and then they *themselves* have to look for some way to reaffirm the values they have overthrown." Yet it is not only the actors who must attempt to find a way to reaffirm fundamental values they have violated in times of great exigency; society must also undertake a project of reaffirmation. Each member of society, in whose name terrible things have been done, must become morally responsible. Such responsibility is assumed by, and through, the process of ratification or rejection of the particular terrible things that have been done "in our name."

Periodical Bibliography

The following articles have been selected to supplement the diverse views presented in this chapter.

Alan M. Dershowitz	"Want to Torture? Get a Warrant," *SFGate*, January 22, 2002. www.sfgate.com.
Gary Feuerberg	"Debate Continues on Executive Powers and Definition of Torture," *Epoch Times*, January 8, 2008. www.theepochtimes.com.
Barton Gellman and Jo Becker	"Pushing the Envelope on Presidential Power," *Washington Post*, June 25, 2007. http://voices.washingtonpost.com.
Fred Kaplan	"Send Him Back to the Bunker!" *Slate.com*, May 21, 2009. www.slate.com.
Glenn Kessler	"Rice Defends Enhanced Interrogations," *Washington Post*, April 30, 2009. http://voices.washingtonpost.com.
Andrew C. McCarthy	"Say 'No' to the McCain Amendment," *National Review Online*, November 15, 2005. www.nationalreview.com.
Barack Obama	"Remarks by the President on National Security," *White House Web site*, May 21, 2009. www.whitehouse.gov.
Jack Rabbit	"Why Torture Doesn't Work: A Critique of Alan Dershowitz' Case for Torture," *Democratic Underground*, March 11, 2004. www.democraticunderground.com.
Andrew Sullivan	"The American Way of Torture, Ctd.," *The Daily Dish*, August 26, 2009. http://andrewsullivan.theatlantic.com.
Philip Watts	"Bush Advisor Says President Has Legal Power to Torture Children," *Information Clearing House*, January 8, 2006. www.informationclearinghouse.info.

CHAPTER 2

How Much Power Should the President Have to Operate in Secret?

Chapter Preface

The government has long kept certain information secret from the public in the interests of national security. However, the amount and kinds of material classified as secret increased substantially after the terrorist attacks of September 11, 2001. The George W. Bush Administration was particularly interested in reducing the scope of the Freedom of Information Act (FOIA), which allows individuals and the press to demand the release of government documents.

Under FOIA, the presumption had been that all federal documents should be released unless there was a reason not to do so. After September 11, 2001, however, the Bush Administration weakened or qualified that presumption. In particular, Attorney General John Ashcroft in an October 12, 2001, memo noted that when federal agencies decided to refuse public access to documents under FOIA, they could "be assured that the Department of Justice will defend your decisions unless they lack a sound legal basis or present an unwarranted risk of adverse impact on the ability of other agencies to protect other important records."

The Bush Administration's aggressive stand on secrecy had a major effect on limiting public access to information. According to John Podesta, former White House chief of staff to President Bill Clinton, in a 2003 essay in *The American Prospect*, classification of documents rose between 2001 and 2003 by 18 percent, and even domestic agencies such as the Department of Agriculture "had been given unprecedented power to classify their own documents." The Bush administration's commitment to secrecy meant that federal spending on paper shredding increased exponentially between 2000 (when shredding costs were $450,000) and 2006 (when shredding costs reached $2.9 million), according to an October 27, 2008, article on radaronline.com. An article on Wired.com from May

28, 2009, showed that the Bush administration also had seen a significant drop in *de*classifying documents; in 1999, 127 million pages were declassified; in 2008 (the last year of the Bush administration) only 31.4 million pages were declassified.

Following his election in 2008, President Barack Obama took some steps to reverse the secrecy policies of the Bush administration. Declaring on May 27, 2009, that "my Administration is committed to operating with an unprecedented level of openness," Obama stated his intention to make it easier for the public to receive information under FOIA requests and to expedite the declassification process.

One of the most dramatic results of the Obama administration's policy was the declassification and release of Bush administration legal memos discussing techniques used in interrogating terrorism suspects. These memos revealed the Bush administration's legal rationale behind the use of so-called enhanced interrogation.

The release of the memos caused much controversy. According to one Bush administration official, the release of the memos was "unbelievable," and damaged national security by preventing the United States from using vital interrogation techniques in the future, Mike Allen reported in an April 16, 2009, article on Politico.com. On the other hand, Glenn Greenwald, a Salon.com blogger who often focuses on civil liberties issues, said that Obama appeared to have done "exactly the right thing" and that the president deserved "real credit." Obama's commitment to openness has its limits, however. In May 2009, he reversed a decision to release pictures showing U.S. abuse of detainees in Iraq at the Abu Ghraib prison. Despite a court order to release the material, Obama took steps to challenge the decision, arguing that making the pictures public could "further inflame anti-American opinion and . . . put our troops in danger," as reported by Scott Wilson on May 14, 2009 in the *Washington Post*. In the same article, a lawyer for the American Civil Liberties Union (ACLU), which had fought to release the photos, said that the decision "renders meaningless President Obama's pledge of transparency and accountability that he made in the early days after taking office."

The authors of the following viewpoints continue this debate about how best to balance secrecy, national security, and the public's need and right to hold the government accountable.

| "The privilege comes at the expense of individual liberty. This tradeoff . . . [may be] necessary to ensure the survival of the very system of government that allows us to pursue those liberty interests in the first place." |

The State Secrets Privilege Is Necessary

Claudio Ochoa

Claudio Ochoa is a lawyer in Washington, D.C. In the following viewpoint, he argues that the state secrets privilege, which allows the executive to withhold information during trials can be a dangerous infringement of both separation of powers and of individual liberties. However, Ochoa argues, these dangers must be balanced against the widely acknowledged fact that national security requires secrecy. Ochoa concludes that the state secrets privilege is a necessary evil.

As you read, consider the following questions:

1. What are some of the most notable invocations of the state secrets privilege by the George W. Bush Administration, according to the author?

Claudio Ochoa, "Federalism and Separation of Powers: The State Secrets Privilege: Necessary Evil?" *Engage*, vol. 8, February 2007, pp. 66–69. Reproduced by permission of the publisher and the author.

2. Who does Claudio Ochoa quote as saying that the invocation of national security borders on being a hoax?

3. According to Ochoa, did George Washington believe that some documents were too secret to give to Congress?

The state secrets privilege . . . allows the Executive to withhold certain information from civil discovery if it believes disclosure would harm the national security or foreign policy of the United States. The privilege is absolute. If a court accepts the Executive's assertion that the subject evidence could reasonably harm the nation's security, the information may not be disclosed regardless how great the need of the party seeking discovery is said to be. In addition to sanctioning sensitive evidence or information in its possession, the Executive can apply the privilege to protect against disclosure of the nation's intelligence gathering sources, methods, and capabilities, and against disruption of diplomatic relations with foreign governments.

The [George W.] Bush Administration has been thoroughly criticized for its use of the privilege, which it has invoked on numerous occasions. The most notable invocations include dismissals of (1) a suit brought by a FBI [Federal Bureau of Investigation] "whistleblower" against the Bureau; (2) a claim that the CIA [Central Intelligence Agency] discriminated against an African-American operations officer because of his race; (3) allegations that CIA operatives kidnapped, tortured and held *incommunicado* a foreign-national until releasing him without charges more than a year later; and (4), most recently, the attempt to prevent judicial review of the National Security Agency's domestic surveillance program.[1] . . .

1. The National Security Agency was tapping phones without warrants.

Criticism of the Privilege

Criticism of the privilege is understandable given its effect on two staples of our system of government: (1) the concept of separation of powers, and (2) the protection of individual rights.

The tension between the privilege and separation of powers was articulated best by the Third Circuit in [*United States vs.*] *Reynolds* [in 1953]:

> But to hold that the head of an executive department of the Government in a suit to which the United States is a party may conclusively determine the Government's claim of privilege is to abdicate the judicial function and permit the executive branch of the Government to infringe the independent province of the judiciary as laid down by the Constitution . . . the Government of the United States is one of checks and balances. One of the principal checks is furnished by the independent judiciary. . . . Neither the executive nor the legislative may encroach upon the field which the Constitution has reserved for the judiciary by transferring to itself the power to decide justiciable questions which arise in cases or controversies submitted to the judicial branch for decision.

Courts have nevertheless been reluctant to scrutinize executive invocations of the privilege because national security matters are uniquely within its expertise. As such, the Executive deserves "the utmost deference." Without a meaningful check-and-balance, though, it is conceivable the Executive could abuse this power to shield information for reasons other than national security. As the Supreme Court noted in *U.S. v. Nixon*, [1974] in its discussion of the President's claim of executive privilege:

> It is but a small step to assert a privilege against any disclosure of records merely because they might prove embarrassing to government officers. Indeed it requires no great flight

of imagination to realize that if the Government's contentions in these cases were affirmed the privilege against disclosure might gradually be enlarged by executive determinations until, as is the case in some nations today, it embraced the whole range of governmental activities.

Despite this warning, courts have tended to grant the Executive significant license to label evidence "secret." This allows it to protect information even for inappropriate purposes—including "to cover up embarrassment, incompetence, corruption or outright violation of law." History is scattered with various examples of such abuse. Some critics claim that the Executive abused the privilege in the very case in which the Supreme Court first formally discussed the privilege, *U.S. v. Reynolds.*

John Dean, former White House Counsel to President Nixon, goes so far as to assert that "the invocation of national security [in state secrets cases] borders on being a hoax." In his opinion, secrets that could harm national security are very rare—most assertions of the privilege are designed to protect embarrassing information and executive overreach of power. As a result, the privilege is "more a sword than a shield," because the government can dispose of a case without litigating the legality of its actions and without having to say exactly why the privilege applies.

Individual Rights

The second critique of the state secrets privilege concerns its effect on individual and constitutional rights. When invoked, the privilege may infringe, if not quash, these rights in the following ways:

1. *Dismissal of legitimate claims:* . . . Because there is no balancing of the merits of a claim versus the importance of the "secret information," courts will dismiss even legitimate and meritorious claims if they accept the

Government's assertion that discovery could reasonably harm national security. In some instances, this could effectively allow executive agencies to "opt out of compliance" with federal statutes by claiming simply that the subject matter touches on issues of national security.

2. *Ex parte communications:*[2] "Justice is rooted in the notion that 'truth will emerge from two advocates presenting their version of the facts in a structured format to a neutral and detached decision-maker.'" But invocation of the privilege often results in ex parte communications between federal officials and the judge, during which the government seeks to persuade the court that issues of national security are at stake. Because opposing counsel often lacks the adequate clearance, counsel may never know the substance of these meetings or the evidence presented by the Government. Additionally, ex parte communications may deny counsel the right to be heard on an issue, as guaranteed by the Sixth and Fourteenth Amendments.[3] . . .

3. "*Blind Counsel*": Private counsel require access to information about their client's case in order to serve as an effective advocate. As a result of ex parte communications, classified evidence, and redacted briefs and opinions, it may be impossible for counsel to know the basis of a court's ruling. "In appealing such a ruling," scholars William Weaver and Robert Pallitto note, "it is unclear how a litigant would be able to go about addressing arguments it may not see, drawn from evidence it may not review."

---

2. Ex parte communications are discussions off the record made to influence an official.
3. The Sixth and Fourteenth amendments to the Constitution cover due process and the rights of the accused.

Obama and State Secrets

Civil liberties advocates are accusing the [Barack] Obama administration of forsaking campaign rhetoric and adopting the same expansive arguments that his predecessor used to cloak some of the most sensitive intelligence-gathering programs of the [George W.] Bush White House.

The first signs have come just weeks into the new administration, in a case filed by an Oregon charity suspected of funding terrorism. President Obama's Justice Department not only sought to dismiss the lawsuit by arguing that it implicated "state secrets," but also escalated the standoff—proposing that government lawyers might take classified documents from the court's custody to keep the charity's representatives from reviewing them.

Carrie Johnson, "Handling of 'State Secrets' at Issue,"
Washington Post, *March 25, 2009. www.washingtonpost.com.*

4. *Substantive rights*: The Bill of Rights guarantees certain rights to each citizen of the United States, such as the right to free speech and protection against unreasonable search and seizure. In some recent cases, plaintiffs have claimed that the Government has infringed on these rights in violation of the Constitution. Yet, by invoking the state secrets privilege, the Executive can shield any alleged constitutional violation from substantive review by a court, regardless of the merits of the claim. In this sense, it appears ultra-constitutional.

Justification for a Strong Privilege

Although these are real and concerning byproducts of the privilege, many argue that they must be considered in conjunction with the privilege's justification.

First and foremost, it is argued, the Executive does not have absolute, un-checked power to invoke the privilege. The privilege is only absolute in the sense that issues of national security will always pre-empt those of the individual. However, before the privilege can reach that point, a court must be satisfied that the case poses a reasonable danger to secrets of state. A court is free to review, question and analyze the Government's assertion until it reaches that level of comfort. It is ultimately up to the court whether to allow its invocation.

Courts have granted the Executive extreme deference in examples where it has been invoked because they themselves have recognized that the Judiciary is ill-equipped to review matters of national security. . . .

This deference may be grounded on a deeper level, as well. There is significant authority for the argument that the President's authority to invoke the privilege is in part based on Article II of the Constitution, not just strictly the common law. It is widely recognized that the President has the "authority to control access to information bearing on national security . . . [which] exists quite apart from any congressional grant. . . . The authority to protect that information falls on the President as head of the Executive Branch and as Commander in Chief." [as stated in *Dept. of Navy vs. Egan* (1988)] In *Nixon*, the Supreme Court "emphasized the heightened status of the President's privilege in the context of 'military, diplomatic, or sensitive national security secrets.'"

Notably, Justice [Potter] Stewart, in his concurrence in *New York Times Co. v. U.S.* [1971], recognized that Executive power in the areas of national defense and international relations were largely unchecked by the legislative and judicial branches. Rather than rein in this power, he concluded: "The responsibility must lie where the power is. If the Constitution gives the Executive a large degree of unshared power in the conduct of foreign affairs and the maintenance of our national defense, then under the Constitution the Executive must have the largely unshared duty to determine and preserve the degree of internal security necessary to exercise that power successfully."

The Founders themselves apparently recognized at least the need for such a privilege. John Jay in *The Federalist Papers* [1787–88] observed hat the only way the Executive could gather valuable intelligence was if it could protect its sources from discovery, even by other branches of the government. [President] George Washington, in deciding whether to turn over documents to the Congress, stated that "he could readily conceive there might be papers of so secret a nature, as that they ought not to be given up." His cabinet, including members Thomas Jefferson and Alexander Hamilton, unanimously agreed that "the Executive ought to communicate such papers as the public good will permit, and ought to refuse those, the disclosure of which would injure the public."

Although all these instances dealt with Executive privilege—withholding documents from Congress or the public at large—there is no reason to believe the state secrets privilege—the withholding of evidence in litigation based on national security concerns—should operate differently. The public, and both the legislative and judicial branches can lay an equal claim on the information. Thus, the genesis of the privilege was not the Cold War, but a recognized need to ensure the continued existence of the country.

Individual Harm, Common Good

At the outset, it must be noted that the state secrets privilege directs dismissal only if the information at issue goes to the core of the claim or a potential defense. It is undeniable that the privilege has a devastating effect on individual litigants who face such a result, but this is an inescapable fact of competing interests. It is often recognized that "[t]he state secrets privilege is the most basic of government privileges [because] it protects the survival of the state, from which all other institutions derive." [according to author and law professor Brian Z. Tamanaha] In other words, the very purpose of the privilege is to serve the common good. And for this reason, the law must render individual interests secondary to the general citizenry, especially in the context of terrorism where there is a significant potential of wide-spread public harm.

The Fourth Circuit directly faced this dilemma in *Sterling v. Tenet* [2005], where the defendant brought a racial discrimination suit against the Director of the Central Intelligence Agency. In dismissing his claim under the Government's invocation of the privilege, the court noted:

> We recognize that our decision places, on behalf of the entire country, a burden on Sterling that he alone must bear. 'When the state secrets privilege is validly asserted, the result is unfairness to individual litigants—through the loss of important evidence or dismissal of a case—in order to protect a greater public value.' Yet there can be no doubt that, in limited circumstances like these, the fundamental principle of access to court must bow to the fact that a nation without sound intelligence is a nation at risk.

Secrecy, although disfavored in a democratic government, has long been held a requisite for any successful intelligence operation. The view was put by George Washington, the first President of the Republic, during his time as General:

> The necessity of procuring good intelligence, is apparent and need not be further urged. All that remains for me to add is, that you keep the whole matter as secret as possible. For upon secrecy, success depends in most enterprises of the kind, and for want of it they are generally defeated.

Further justification of the privilege is made on the grounds that not only is secrecy necessary to gain valuable intelligence to protect Americans but also in ensuring that the very methods used to secure that information not be compromised. According to the current administration, "disclosure of this information 'would enable adversaries of the United States to avoid detection from the nation's intelligence activities, sources, and methods, and/or take measures to defeat or neutralize those activities thus, seriously damaging the United States' national security interests.'" To give a plaintiff or even a group of plaintiffs the power to force the Executive to disclose details about secret informants, operations, or programs (including those that have been successful in gathering information or preventing attacks)—thereby compromising their integrity, and the safety of American citizens—would "convert the constitutional Bill of Rights into a suicide pact." [according to attorney Adam J. White] . . .

For these reasons, it can well be argued that the privilege is neither undemocratic nor a relic of the Cold War. Due [to] the drastic effect it has on litigants each time it is invoked, it is also evident, however, that the privilege comes at the expense of individual liberty. This tradeoff, always distasteful, may in the end be necessary to ensure the survival of the very system of government that allows us to pursue those liberty interests in the first place.

"By using the state secrets privilege to shut down whole lawsuits . . . the administration avoids having to give a legal account of its behavior."

The State Secrets Privilege Is Dangerous

Henry Lanman

Henry Lanman is a lawyer in New York City. In the following viewpoint, he argues that the state secrets privilege was traditionally used to exclude evidence that might threaten national security. By contrast, he maintains, the George W. Bush administration used the privilege to shut down entire cases. In some of these cases, Lanman argues, the information at issue was not even secret, but was publicly known. Thus, Lanman contends, the state secrets privilege has become a means whereby the executive can avoid scrutiny of its potentially illegal actions.

As you read, consider the following questions:

1. How many times did the George W. Bush Administration assert the state secrets privilege in the four years after September 11, 2001, according to the author?

Henry Lanman, "Secret Guarding," Slate.com, May 22, 2006. Reproduced by permission.

2. On what grounds does Henry Lanman argue that the state secrets privilege was misused in *United States v. Reynolds?*

3. In the case of *Hepting v. AT&T*, what did the plaintiffs claim AT&T had done, according to Lanman?

Last Thursday [May 18, 2006], a federal court in Virginia threw out a lawsuit against the government that had been brought by a German citizen named Khalid el-Masri. El-Masri alleged that the government had violated U.S. law when—as part if its "extraordinary rendition"[1] program—it authorized his abduction, drugging, confinement, and torture. His captors allegedly shuttled him on clandestine flights to and from places like Kabul, Baghdad, and Skopje, Macedonia, during the five months of his detention. He was released only when the government realized it had kidnapped the wrong man. El-Masri has substantial evidence to back up his story, and German prosecutors have verified much of it. And, while the government has not confirmed that it took el-Masri as part of its extraordinary rendition program, it has not shied away from admitting the program exists; it has in fact trumpeted it as an effective tool in the "war on terror." So why then was el-Masri's lawsuit thrown out? Because the judge accepted the government's claim that any alleged activities relating to el-Masri were "state secrets."

Overuse

Never heard of the "state secrets" privilege? You're not alone. But the [George W.] Bush administration sure has. Before [the terrorist attacks of] Sept. 11 [2001] this obscure privilege was invoked only rarely. Since then, the administration has dramatically increased its use. According to the *Washington Post*, the Reporters' Committee for Freedom of the Press reported

---

1. Extraordinary rendition is the government program of shipping prisoners to secret locations in other countries.

that while the government asserted the privilege approximately 55 times in total between 1954 (the privilege was first recognized in 1953) and 2001, it's asserted it 23 times in the four years after Sept. 11. For an administration as obsessed with secrecy as this one is, the privilege is simply proving to be too powerful a tool to pass up.

There is nothing inherently objectionable about the state secrets privilege. It recognizes the reasonable proposition that even simple lawsuits against the government—tort suits, breach of contract claims—can sometimes involve issues that would be genuinely harmful to national security if they saw the light of day. Say, for instance, that a janitor in Los Alamos, N.M., tripped over a box of uranium lying in the hallway in 1943. It would hardly do to have the evidence used in the subsequent slip-and-fall case scuttle the entire Manhattan Project.[2] So, tough though it is on individual plaintiffs, the courts have historically deferred claims that some evidence in certain litigation must be shielded as "state secrets."

Traditionally, this privilege was most often used to prevent plaintiffs from getting a hold of very specific, sensitive evidence in an ongoing lawsuit; it was seldom invoked to dismiss entire cases. Maybe that hypothetical Los Alamos plaintiff couldn't have discovered exactly what was in the box that he tripped over. But, generally speaking, if the lawsuit could have proceeded without his knowing the contents of that box, it would.

The troubling shift today is that in *el-Masri* and other similar lawsuits—almost all of which involve important challenges to the government's conduct since Sept. 11—the administration has been routinely asserting the privilege to dismiss the suits in their entirety by claiming that for it to participate in the trials at all would mean revealing state secrets. In other words, in addition to relying on the state secrets doctrine to an unprecedented degree, the administration

---

2. The Manhattan Project was the U.S. program to develop an atomic bomb.

is now well on its way to transforming it from a narrow evidentiary privilege into something that looks like a doctrine of broad government immunity.

The state secrets privilege has proved to be such an enticing tool for the Bush administration largely because courts have historically been very deferential to the government's secrecy claims. According to an analysis by William Weaver and Robert Pallitto, political science professors at the University of Texas-El Paso, courts have examined the documents' underlying claims of state secrecy fewer than one-third of the times it has been invoked. And, according to their review, courts have only actually rejected the assertion of the privilege four times since 1953.

The compliant nature of the judiciary here is not completely surprising. Judges are understandably reluctant to second-guess government claims about something as important as national security, perhaps rightly so. But this reluctance does have consequences. If the courts don't keep the executive honest, the only check is the executive's self-restraint, which, we are coming to learn, can't always be counted upon.

Misuse

Indeed, *United States v. Reynolds*, the Supreme Court decision first recognizing the legitimacy of a state secrets privilege, is also apparently an object lesson in how the privilege can be misused. Decided in 1953 at the height of the Cold War, *Reynolds* was brought by the widows of three civilians who died when the Air Force plane they were on crashed. The widows sued the Air Force for negligently maintaining the aircraft and tried to obtain accident reports from the government to further their suit. Unfortunately for the widows, in addition to their husbands, the plane was also carrying secret electronic equipment. Citing the presence of this top-secret equipment, the government refused to turn over the documents, claiming

Statement of Khaled El-Masri

Almost one year ago [in 2006] the American Civil Liberties Union, on my behalf, filed a lawsuit against George Tenet, the former director of the CIA. . . . For reasons I do not fully understand, the court decided not to hear my case because the government claimed that allowing the case to proceed would reveal state secrets, even though the facts of my mistreatment have been widely reported in American and international media.

This is not democracy. In my opinion, this is how you establish a dictatorial regime. Countries are occupied, people are killed, and we cannot say anything because it's all considered a state secret. Freedom and justice are disrespected, as are basic morals and values. And if you don't keep quiet after you are abused, you are considered a threat to international or national security. But I will not be scared into silent.

Khaled El-Masri,
"Statement: Khaled El-Masri,"
American Civil Liberties Union. www.aclu.org.

that doing so would jeopardize national security. The Supreme Court upheld the government's refusal, and the state secrets privilege was born.

As it turns out, the documents didn't really back up the Air Force's claims. In 2000, the children of the original plaintiffs got hold of the reports their mothers sought when the documents became declassified. Nothing in these documents appeared to bear at all on national security. They were, however, filled with evidence of negligence, all of which was nicely summarized by the Air Force's straightforward conclusion that "the aircraft is not considered to have been safe for flight."

In addition to the fact that the government is using what was once largely an evidentiary privilege to dismiss entire lawsuits, the administration's sweeping use of the *Reynolds* privilege is disturbing because it's also using it to dismiss even those lawsuits in which the underlying facts have already received substantial publicity.

Not Even Secret

Take, for instance, *Hepting v. AT&T* [2006], which arises out of the NSA's [National Security Agency] warrantless wiretap program.[3] It's a class-actions suit, brought on behalf of AT&T's customers who claim that the company violated various laws when it allegedly gave the NSA access to its facilities and databases. As part of their case, the plaintiffs have submitted 140 pages of technical documents that, they say, lay out how AT&T's collaboration with the NSA works. The government doesn't claim that these documents are classified. Yet when the *New York Times*—which also has copies of these documents—showed them to telecommunications and computer security experts, these experts concluded that the documents themselves demonstrate that "AT&T had an agreement with the federal government to systematically gather information flowing on the Internet through the company's network." And, of course, the president himself has acknowledged the existence of the warrantless surveillance program.

That makes it awfully hard to understand how the core claims in this case—basically that the program exists and that AT&T participates in it—are so top-secret that, as the administration has claimed in its papers, the whole case must be dismissed before it gets started. Of course, it's not unimaginable that real state secrets could arise in this lawsuit, but if they did, there's no reason to think they couldn't be handled the same way such issues have been in the past—as discrete evidentiary matters. However, even this level of skepticism from

---

3. The NSA ran a program where it tapped people's phones without obtaining warrants.

the judiciary may be too much to ask; the court hearing El-Masri's case just rejected essentially the same argument.

Despite the burgeoning use of this privilege and the way it's been used to gut entire cases, the most disturbing aspect of the Bush administration's expansion of the state secrets privilege may well be this: More and more, it is invoked not in response to run-of-the-mill government negligence cases but in response to allegations of criminal conduct on the part of the government. These are not slip-and-fall cases. They are challenges to the administration's broad new theories of unchecked executive power. By using the state secrets privilege to shut down whole lawsuits that would examine government actions before the cases even get under way, the administration avoids having to give a legal account of its behavior. And if this tactic persists—if the administration continues to broadly assert this privilege and courts continue to accept it—the administration will have succeeded in creating an insurmountable immunity that can be invoked against pretty much any legal claim that the "war on terror" violates the law. The standard and winning response to any plaintiff who asserted such charges would be, quite simply, that it's a secret.

The Bush administration has fought at every turn to limit scrutiny of its conduct since Sept. 11 [2001]. And, unless courts start to reject its assertion, the administration may have found in the state secrets privilege the ultimate tool for making its actions invisible.

> *"The courts repeatedly recognized the president's constitutional power to conduct warrantless wiretapping."*

Warrantless Wiretapping Is Necessary and Legal

Andrew C. McCarthy

Andrew C. McCarthy, a former federal prosecutor, is a senior fellow at the Foundation for the Defense of Democracies. In the following viewpoint, McCarthy argues that presidents have the constructional authority to request warrantless wiretaps. Furthermore, McCarthy argues that even if President George W. Bush had gone to the court created by the 1978 Foreign Intelligence Surveillance Act to request authorization for wiretaps, there still would have been a scandal. The heart of the scandal, McCarthy insists, has nothing to do with the legalities of warrantless wiretapping, and those suggesting otherwise are putting our national security at risk.

As you read, consider the following questions:

1. Does Andrew C. McCarthy believe the president has the constitutional authority to grant warrantless wiretaps?

2. Why does the author believe what he refers to as a "domestic spying scandal" was created?

3. What does McCarthy believe questions about the legalities of warrantless wiretapping obscure?

For the frivolous, war is scandal fodder any which way you choose.

FISA Compliance

What if President [George W.] Bush had actually gone to the court created by the 1978 Foreign Intelligence Surveillance Act [FISA]?

Imagine if, instead of relying on his own constitutional authority, he had done the thing his detractors now insist he should have done. That is, what if he had actually gone to the FISA court and requested authorization to eavesdrop on Americans suspected of helping al Qaeda wage its terrorist war against the United States?

Now, let's suppose the same brave, anonymous "whistle-blowers"—in the same sort of flagrant violation of federal law and of the oath of confidentiality they gave to be trusted with access to the nation's most sensitive information—had instead leaked *that* program. Let's suppose they had gone to James Risen of the *New York Times* and told him not about warrantless wiretapping but about a surge in eavesdropping under judicial imprimatur.

Would that FISA compliance have made it all okay? Do you really think there would have been no scandal?

Or, in this climate that it has so tirelessly labored to create, do you think the *Times* would simply have weaved a different scandal?

We are talking, after all, about the newspaper that is now "of record" only if you're keeping track of the hard Left's daily scripts—the trailblazer of an era in which politicizing our national security during wartime, once unthinkable, is everyday fare. We are talking about a crowd that never met a savage they wouldn't Mirandize [read Miranda warning; to inform a suspect of his legal rights] or a library they wouldn't turn into a safe haven for plotting mass murder.

Would the *Times* and the rest of the shock troops really be saying the same things they are piously declaiming now? Would we still be hearing: "Of course we believe in aggressively fighting terrorists. Of course we need to root out those collaborating with terrorists. We fully support that, as long as it's done within the Rule of Law"?

Or would we be hearing something altogether different?

Domestic Spying Scandal?

Once it had sat on the story for a year, biding its time for the right opportunity to drop the bomb—say, right as the Patriot Act was about to be voted on, or right as the administration was basking in the glow of a successful Iraqi election—is there a snowball's chance on West 43rd Street [in New York City] that the Gray Lady [nickname for the *New York Times*] would not have just tinkered with a few adjectives and, *presto!*, manufactured a domestic spying scandal all the same?

That's not the scandal we have. So, sure, let's talk until we're blue in the face about the abstruse legalities of warrantless wiretapping. Have the courts repeatedly recognized the president's constitutional power to conduct warrantless wiretapping? Does the president have the power regardless of whether the courts acknowledge it? Can Congress, by passing a statute like FISA, limit the president's commander-in-chief prerogatives? Is FISA unconstitutional, at least at the margins? Is FISA, in any event, too bureaucratically sclerotic to combat a nimble foe like al Qaeda? Could the administration have avoided controversy by asking Congress to amend FISA? Or by using FISA's provision for retroactive judicial approval within 72 hours of emergency eavesdropping?

The President Can Declare War

Question: Presidents have often sought a legislative stamp of approval for engaging in wars—for instance, the current war with Iraq and the 1991 Gulf War. Do you think the reasons for that are entirely political, or is there a legal reason for seeking that approval?

[John] Yoo: I do not think that the president is constitutionally required to get legislative authorization for launching military hostilities, and presidents from [Harry] Truman through [Bill] Clinton have not done so. But I think that there are complicated political reasons why presidents have gone to Congress recently for support. The wars in Iraq and Afghanistan were approved by Congress, and President [George W.] Bush sought that support while at the same time claiming he had the constitutional power to launch the wars anyway. Presidents seek such support for two reasons: first, to send a signal to the enemy that the United States is serious about its intentions to go to war, and second, to maintain political unity by getting members of Congress on the record before the war starts, so that they cannot claim after the war that they did not agree with it.

"An Interview with John Yoo,"
University of Chicago Press, *2005.*
www.press.uchicago.edu.

The Bottom Line

But the exhaustion of these questions, in the self-conscious pomp of serious discussion, mustn't obscure what is really going on here. This, plain and simple, is a political game of "Gotcha!" Played with our national security—played with the lives of the innocent.

For serious people, wartime decisions are sober, often excruciating choices between liberty and security. But for those not invested in America's victory over our highly motivated, highly committed enemies, they can be spun into high crimes no matter which choices are made.

And for those whose agenda, far from victory, is vengeance for the [Bill] Clinton impeachment, they will continue to be spun just that way until that beloved "Mission Accomplished" banner is draped, finally, over the remains of the Bush presidency.

We can politely pretend otherwise. But that's what this "scandal" is about. And what the next one will be about.

| "This program is breaking the law, and this President is breaking the law."

Warrantless Wiretapping Is Illegal and Unconstitutional

Russell Feingold

Russell Feingold is a Democratic U.S. Senator from Wisconsin. In the following viewpoint, he argues that wiretapping without a warrant violates the Constitution. He says wiretapping is necessary, but that it should be done legally with a warrant issued by an independent judge. Feingold contends that this is especially true since the George W. Bush Administration has shown itself to be untrustworthy by its false statements before the 2003 invasion of Iraq. Feingold concludes that the president has violated the law and must be held accountable by Congress.

As you read, consider the following questions:

1. According to Russell Feingold, which Constitutional amendment is violated by warrantless wiretapping?

2. When did the president declare "Mission Accomplished" in Iraq, according to the author?

Russell Feingold, "Bush's Warrantless Wiretapping Program Is Illegal and Unconstitutional," *Counterpunch*, February 8, 2006.

3. Feingold says that what committee held hearings on the domestic spying program?

Last week [January 31, 2006], the President of the United States [George W. Bush] gave his State of the Union address, where he spoke of America's leadership in the world, and called on all of us to "lead this world toward freedom." Again and again, he invoked the principle of freedom, and how it can transform nations, and empower people around the world.

Violating Basic Freedoms

But, almost in the same breath, the President openly acknowledged that he has ordered the government to spy on Americans, on American soil, without the warrants required by law.

The President issued a call to spread freedom throughout the world, and then he admitted that he has deprived Americans of one of their most basic freedoms under the Fourth Amendment—to be free from unjustified government intrusion.[1]

The President was blunt. He said that he had authorized the NSA's[2] domestic spying program, and he made a number of misleading arguments to defend himself. His words got rousing applause from Republicans, and even some Democrats.

The President was blunt, so I will be blunt: This program is breaking the law, and this President is breaking the law. Not only that, he is misleading the American people in his efforts to justify this program.

How is that worthy of applause? Since when do we celebrate our commander in chief for violating our most basic freedoms, and misleading the American people in the process?

1. The 4th Amendment outlaws unreasonable searches.
2. The NSA, or National Security Agency, operated a program of warrantless wiretaps.

Lies and Iraq

Each year of George W. Bush's war in Iraq has been represented by a thematic falsehood. That Iraq is now calm or more stable is only the latest in a series of such whoppers, which the mainstream press eagerly repeats. The fifth anniversary [in 2008] of Bush's invasion of Iraq will be the last he presides. Sen. John McCain [the Republican nominee for president in 2008.], in turn, has now taken to dangling the bait of total victory before the American public, and some opinion polls suggest that Americans are swallowing it, hook, line and sinker.

The most famous falsehoods connected to the war were those deployed by the president and his close advisors to justify the invasion. But each of the subsequent years since U.S. troops barreled toward Baghdad in March 2003 has been marked by propaganda campaigns just as mendacious.

Juan Cole, "Five years of Iraq Lies,"
Salon.com, *March 19, 2008. www.salon.com.*

When did we start to stand up and cheer for breaking the law? In that moment at the State of the Union, I felt ashamed.

Congress has lost its way if we don't hold this President accountable for his actions.

Wiretap Within the Law

The President suggests that anyone who criticizes his illegal wiretapping program doesn't understand the threat we face. But we do. Every single one of us is committed to stopping the terrorists who threaten us and our families.

Defeating the terrorists should be our top national priority, and we all agree that we need to wiretap them to do it. In fact, it would be irresponsible not to wiretap terrorists. But we have yet to see any reason why we have to trample the laws of the United States to do it. The President's decision that he can break the law says far more about his attitude toward the rule of law than it does about the laws themselves.

This goes way beyond party, and way beyond politics. What the President has done here is to break faith with the American people. In the State of the Union, he also said that "we must always be clear in our principles" to get support from friends and allies that we need to fight terrorism. So let's be clear about a basic American principle: When someone breaks the law, when someone misleads the public in an attempt to justify his actions, he needs to be held accountable. The President of the United States has broken the law. The President of the United States is trying to mislead the American people. And he needs to be held accountable.

Unfortunately, the President refuses to provide any details about this domestic spying program. Not even the full Intelligence committees [of Congress] know the details, and they were specifically set up to review classified information and oversee the intelligence activities of our government. Instead, the President says "Trust me."

Not Trustworthy

This is not the first time we've heard that. In the lead-up to the Iraq war, the Administration went on an offensive to get the American public, the Congress, and the international community to believe its theory that Saddam Hussein[3] was developing weapons of mass destruction, and even that he had ties to Al Qaeda. The President painted a dire and inaccurate picture of Saddam Hussein's capability and intent, and we invaded Iraq on that basis. To make matters worse, the Administration misled the country about what it would take to

3. Saddam Hussein was the leader of Iraq.

stabilize and reconstruct Iraq after the conflict. We were led to believe that this was going to be a short endeavor, and that our troops would be home soon.

We all recall the President's "Mission Accomplished" banner on the aircraft carrier on May 1, 2003. In fact, the mission was not even close to being complete. More than 2,100 total deaths have occurred after the President declared an end to major combat operations in May of 2003, and over 16,600 American troops have been wounded in Iraq. The President misled the American people and grossly miscalculated the true challenge of stabilizing and rebuilding Iraq.

In December [2005], we found out that the President has authorized wiretaps of Americans without the court orders required by law. He says he is only wiretapping people with links to terrorists, but how do we know? We don't. The President is unwilling to let a neutral judge make sure that is the case. He will not submit this program to an independent branch of government to make sure he's not violating the rights of law-abiding Americans.

So I don't want to hear again that this Administration has shown it can be trusted. It hasn't. And that is exactly why the law requires a judge to review these wiretaps.

It is up to Congress to hold the President to account. We held a hearing on the domestic spying program in the [senate] Judiciary Committee yesterday [February 6, 2006], where attorney General [Alberto] Gonzales was a witness. We expect there will be other hearings. That is a start, but it will take more than just hearings to get the job done.

Periodical Bibliography

The following articles have been selected to supplement the diverse views presented in this chapter.

Lyle Denniston	"President's Power to Detain in U.S. at Issue," *Scotusblog*, October 27, 2007. www.scotusblog.com.
Lawrence Friedman and Victor Hansen	"Closing Time: Presidential Power and Emergencies," *JURIST*, January 28, 2009. http://jurist.law.pitt.edu.
Beth George	"Reforming the State Secrets Privilege," *Legal Workshop*, October 30, 2009. www.legalworkshop.org.
Glenn Greenwald	"The 180-degree Reversal of Obama's State Secrets Position," *Salon.com*, February 10, 2009. www.salon.com.
Bill Hayman	"Conservatives Challenge Presidential Power Grab, Demand Reforms to Restore Checks and Balances," *American Chronicle*, March 21, 2007. www.americanchronicle.com.
Shayana Kadidal	"Forum: The State Secrets Privilege and Executive Misconduct," *JURIST*, May 30, 2006. http://jurist.law.pitt.edu.
David Kravets	"Obama Sides with Bush in Spy Case," *Threat Level*, January 22, 2009. www.wired.com.
Tom A. Peter	"Bush Wants Permanent Warrantless Wiretap Law," *Christian Science Monitor*, September 21, 2007. www.csmonitor.com.
James Risen and Eric Litchtblau	"Bush Lets U.S. Spy on Callers without Courts," *New York Times*, December 16, 2005. www.nytimes.com.
Jake Tapper	"Obama Administration Invokes State Secrets Privilege . . . Again," *Political Punch*, October 30, 2009. http://blogs.abcnews.com.

CHAPTER 3

To What Extent Should the President Be Constrained by Domestic Law?

Chapter Preface

In the American Constitution, there is a balance of power among the president (the executive branch), the Congress (the legislative branch), and the judicial branch. However, some commentators have argued that during a time of national emergency, the president's powers should be vastly expanded to enable quick and decisive action and to preserve the nation's safety.

One of the most aggressive voices arguing for broad presidential powers in an emergency has been John Yoo, an official in the U.S. Department of Justice during the George W. Bush Administration. Yoo helped draft opinions arguing that the United States was not bound by the Geneva Conventions, which are international treaties regulating the conduct of armed conflict. In addition, he argued that the United States could engage in so called "enhanced interrogation techniques," or torture, in certain situations.

Yoo has gone even further than this, however. In his 2006 book *The Powers of War and Peace: The Constitution and Foreign Affairs after 9/11*, he maintained that the president has the sole power to send troops into war. Even though the Constitution says that Congress has the power to "declare war," Yoo in an interview on the University of Chicago Press Web site maintained that practically speaking, "Declarations of war do not serve a purpose in the balance of powers between the president and Congress in wartime." Yoo noted, "I do not think that the president is constitutionally required to get legislative authorization for launching military hostilities, and presidents from (Harry) Truman through (Bill) Clinton have not done so." Yoo also argued that no international law can bind the United States in the way or manner in which it wages war.

Other writers have vigorously disagreed with Yoo's interpretation of the Constitution and the president's war powers. David Cole, writing in the November 17, 2005, issue of *The New York Review of Books*, argued that Yoo had misread the evidence, and that in fact "the Constitution gave the president only the power, as commander in chief, to carry out defensive wars when the country came under attack, and to direct operations in wars that Congress authorized." Moreover, Cole said, Congress should have the power to declare war in order to reduce the likelihood of war. "As the framers accurately predicted," Cole noted, "presidents have proven much more eager than Congress to involve the nation in wars," in part, Cole suggests, because "Presidents . . . tend to benefit from war more than members of Congress, by increasing their short-term popularity, by acquiring broader powers over both the civilian economy and the armed forces, and, sometimes, by the historical recognition later accorded them."

The following viewpoints examine other situations in which the power of the president may or may not be restrained by the power of Congress and by laws in the interest of national security and civil liberties.

"In some limited and relatively rare circumstances, the President might best fulfill his constitutional obligation by refusing to enforce a statutory provision that he considers to be unconstitutional."

Signing Statements Are Reasonable in Some Cases

David Barron, Walter Dellinger, Dawn Johnsen, Neil Kinkopf, Marty Lederman, Chris Schroeder, Richard Shiffrin, and Michael Small

The authors of this viewpoint are all lawyers who have served in the Office of Legal Counsel to the President. In the following viewpoint, they argue that a president should not have to choose between enforcing an unconstitutional provision of a law and vetoing an entire bill. The authors maintain that signing statements, in which a president states his belief that some portion of a law is unconstitutional and that he may not enforce it in some situations, provide a useful third option. The authors argue, however, that signing statements should be rare and limited, and that the George W. Bush Administration misused them.

David Barron, Walter Dellinger, Dawn Johnsen, Neil Kinkopf, Marty Lederman, Chris Schroeder, Richard Shiffrin, and Michael Small, "Untangling the Debate on Signing Statements," Georgetown Law Faculty Blog, July 31, 2006. Reproduced by permission of the authors.

As you read, consider the following questions:

1. What did the McCain Amendment prohibit, according to the authors?

2. What act did President Franklin D. Roosevelt sign even though he believed one of its provisions was unconstitutional?

3. According to the authors, did the McCain Amendment become law despite the signing statement?

President [George W.] Bush has made extensive use of signing statements[1] to announce his constitutional doubts about numerous statutory enactments and to signal his intent either to refuse to enforce such laws or to construe and implement them in a manner consistent with his constitutional views. . . .

Enforcing Unconstitutional Laws

The American Bar Association [ABA] recently joined the debate with the release of a Report by a bipartisan task force on presidential signing statements and the separation of powers. . . . A number of aspects of the Report are very timely and worthwhile. In particular, we agree with the Report's emphasis on the need for transparency whenever the executive branch declines to execute a statute or construes that statute in a manner that appears to be contrary to its text and congressional intent. But we were surprised by, and disagree with, certain of the Report's central conclusions, namely:

1. that "the 'take care' obligation of the President requires him to faithfully execute all laws," including, apparently, those that are unconstitutional; and

1. A signing statement is a statement added to a bill by a president declaring his intention not to enforce part of it, usually on constitutional grounds.

2. that if a President believes any provision of a bill is unconstitutional, he is obliged either (a) to veto the entire bill, or (b) to sign the bill and enforce the unconstitutional provisions.

As we explain below, the first conclusion is untenable. There is a long history of Presidents concluding that, in certain limited circumstances, it is more consistent with their constitutional obligations to refuse to enforce an unconstitutional law than to enforce it. As just the most obvious example, some laws might be plainly unconstitutional under governing and uncontroverted Supreme Court precedent. We do not believe there is a serious case to be made for a constitutional obligation to enforce all such provisions.

But the main target of the ABA Report appears to be not so much these easy cases, but instead cases such as the recent [December 2005] McCain Amendment categorically prohibiting the cruel treatment of prisoners in U.S. custody. President Bush signed the omnibus appropriations bill of which this provision was one small part and at the same time issued a signing statement obliquely suggesting that he may reserve the power to make exceptions pursuant to his authority as Commander-in-Chief.

There are serious problems with the views expressed in such Bush signing statements, but the Report misses the mark in identifying them. Like most misdiagnoses, the Report may have the doubly negative effect of concentrating attention on a phony problem—the issuance of signing statements that long have been used to signal the President's belief that some aspect of a piece of legislation is unconstitutional—while at the same time deflecting attention from a very real problem, namely, the unjustifiable arrogation [or appropriation] of power that President Bush has asserted and continues to assert in office. Below we identify . . . common objections to the use of signing statements (not all of them directly attributable to the ABA Report) and explain why they are misplaced. . . .

Misplaced Objections

First, and most importantly, some objections to recent signing statements appear to be premised on the notion that the President is categorically prohibited from refusing to enforce a statute that he determines to be unconstitutional. But such a categorical prohibition is belied by a long history of Presidents declining, in certain limited circumstances, to enforce statutes that they deem unconstitutional. . . .

To be sure, the ABA Report is correct that the practice has increased in modern times, and some of that increase can be attributed to presidential abuse. But much of the increase is a function of Congress's increased use of omnibus legislation that includes, among literally hundreds of constitutionally unobjectionable provisions, a handful of provisions that might be unconstitutional, including some that are clearly invalid under governing Supreme Court precedent. In such cases, at the very least, a refusal to enforce has been and should continue to be uncontroversial.

We agree wholeheartedly that a President cannot simply choose not to enforce whichever statutes he does not like. A President may not exercise a dispensing power—in effect a type of "line-item-veto"—to ignore statutes that he thinks are unwise, or wrong, or politically inexpedient. . . . The President has an obligation under Article II [of the Constitution] to faithfully execute the laws.

But that "Take Care" obligation includes a responsibility, above all, to faithfully execute the Constitution. Thus, in some limited and relatively rare circumstances, the President might best fulfill his constitutional obligation by refusing to enforce a statutory provision that he considers to be unconstitutional.

This decidedly does not mean that the President can or should always choose noncompliance every time his personal view is that a particular provision is unconstitutional. . . .

A Rare Option

Accordingly, we are on common ground with the ABA Task Force in several important respects, namely:

- Nonenforcement should never be the President's first resort when met with a constitutionally dubious statute—and should rarely be the last resort, either. The Bush Administration's seemingly cavalier assertions of the authority to refuse to enforce laws as Congress has written them places it at odds with its predecessors of both political parties.

- The President is obliged to work diligently with Congress to eliminate any constitutional doubts during the legislative process. . . .

- The President, like a court, should treat Congress's contrary constitutional judgment seriously, and begin analysis of a statute with a presumption of constitutionality. . . .

- The Supreme Court has a special role in establishing constitutional meaning in our system, and therefore the President should rarely refuse to enforce a law without some confidence that doing so would not be inconsistent with the Court's own views.

- And, relatedly, . . . the President should typically act in a way that promotes judicial resolution of the constitutional dispute between the political branches. The option of enforcement and then a refusal to defend should always be carefully considered as a default rule, even if . . . that fallback might always be the optimal solution.

Briefly summarized, we think nonenforcement on any seriously contested question of constitutional law should be the rare exception, a rule of thumb that coincides with Executive practice prior to this Administration.

In contrast, the view that nonenforcement on constitutional grounds should be condemned under any circumstances strikes us as not only historically anomalous, but untenable, particularly in light of the ever-growing number of clearly unconstitutional statutory provisions duly enacted by Congress and sitting on the books. Should [President Thomas] Jefferson really have permitted sedition prosecutions to continue? Should the Executive branch enforce criminal laws, still on the books, that make it unlawful to distribute information about abortions? Enforce social-security and welfare laws that discriminate on the basis of sex in a manner patently inconsistent with Supreme Court case law? . . . How would such enforcement possibly constitute faithful execution of the Constitution?

Not the Statement, but the Enforcement

Second, despite all the negative attention that signing statements have received in the past months, there is nothing inherently wrong with signing statements as such—including those that contain constitutional objections. Thus, for example, the statement of the ABA President when he unveiled the Report last week—that "the threat to our Republic posed by presidential signing statements is both imminent and real unless immediate corrective action is taken"—misses the point. . . .

There is absolutely nothing unlawful about any signing statement. The constitutional problem arises when the President executes, or fails to execute, a statute.

Presidents have used such statements throughout our history. As Walter Dellinger [one of the authors of this viewpoint] explained in another OLC[2] memo:

> [S]uch statements may on appropriate occasions perform useful and legally significant functions. These functions in-

2. The OLC, or Office of Legal Counsel, provides legal advice to the executive branch and the president.

clude (1) explaining to the public, and particularly to constituencies interested in the bill, what the President believes to be the likely effects of its adoption, (2) directing subordinate officers within the Executive Branch how to interpret or administer the enactment, and (3) informing Congress and the public that the Executive believes that a particular provision would be unconstitutional in certain of its applications, or that it is unconstitutional on its face, and that the provision will not be given effect by the Executive Branch to the extent that such enforcement would create an unconstitutional condition.

Dellinger's third category—a statement announcing the intent not to enforce an unconstitutional provision—obviously is the most controversial. But again, it's hardly unprecedented.

Indeed, the ABA Report gets it exactly backwards. The signing statement is a good thing: a manifestation of the Executive's intentions that helps us to understand the heart of the problem. If the President has decided to decline to enforce a statute because it's unconstitutional (. . .) then it is much better that he tell the Congress and the public of his intentions, rather than keep it secret, because in that case the checks and balances of the constitutional system can be set to work.

A Binary Choice

A close reading of the ABA Report suggests, however, that the Task Force's real concern is not so much the signing statement, as such, but a purported constitutional failure at the moment of presentment. The Task Force view appears to be that if a President is presented with a bill that he knows contains an unconstitutional provision he has a binary choice: veto it or sign it and enforce it fully. . . .

There is an intuitive appeal to this notion. After all, if the President determines that a bill presented to him contains an unconstitutional provision, doesn't he have an obligation un-

Obama Negates Signing Statements

President Barack Obama is essentially nullifying hundreds of so-called signing statements in which George W. Bush took issue with provisions in bills he signed.

Bush used signing statements to express opposition to about 1,200 items in legislation passed during his eight years in office. In many instances, he told federal agencies they should ignore the offending provisions because they intruded on duties he said the Constitution reserved exclusively for the executive branch.

On Monday [March 9, 2009], Obama issued a memorandum . . . telling agencies not to follow on them without consulting with the Justice Department in advance.

Josh Gerstein,
"Obama: Ignore Signing Statements,"
Politico, *March 9, 2009. www.politico.com.*

der the Take Care Clause to veto the bill, rather than to sign it and then refuse to enforce the provision?

We believe there is such an obligation if the entire bill is facially unconstitutional.

But that doesn't describe the recurring problem in modern government. Much more often, the constitutionally objectionable provisions are included in important omnibus bills, such as an appropriations bill, containing numerous other valuable or essential provisions. And it is with respect to these omnibus bills that Presidents generally have resorted to the signing statement and nonenforcement, rather than using the veto.

One example: President [Franklin D.] Roosevelt signed the Lend Lease Act, despite his conclusion that one of its provisions was unconstitutional, because he believed the Act vital to the success of World War II. The provision he believed unconstitutional authorized Congress to rescind, by concurrent resolution, specified authorities granted to the President. President Roosevelt's constitutional interpretation was vindicated over 40 years later in *INS v. Chadha*. Congress continues to this day repeatedly to enact provisions that seek to expand congressional power in violation of *Chadha*.

One might argue that this longstanding practice should be nipped in the bud—that Congress should be deterred from including such constitutionally dubious provisions in important omnibus bills and that a series of vetoes is just the way to do it. Perhaps that would be a salutary development, but we do not think the Constitution compels such a result.

The Task Force suggests that the Presentment Clause[3] prohibits the President from using such signing statements. But that concern is off the mark. When the President signs a bill presented to him it becomes positive law—all of it, even the constitutionally objectionable provisions—and thus the Presentment Clause is satisfied. The fact that the President asserts a right not to enforce it does not mean that it is wiped off the books. There is, in other words, no "line-item veto." An example should prove the point: If President Bush had had the power to "line-item veto" the McCain Amendment, it would never have become law, and would never have bound federal interrogation practices. But because he did not veto it, it is an actual statute: It binds the conduct of executive branch actors in the absence of a presidential directive not to enforce it, and it can and will be enforced by future Presidents who disagree with President Bush's view of the Commander-in-Chief Clause (or if the Supreme Court were to declare that it is constitutional).

Signing Statements

Moreover, even if one thinks that it would be good policy for the President to veto all bills containing unconstitutional pro-

3. The Presentment clause refers to Article 1, Section 7, Clauses 2 and 3 of the U.S. Constitution, which describes how bills become law.

visions, it will never happen. Presidents will not begin to veto finely wrought and hard-fought legislation of any importance just because two or three provisions out of a thousand contain a *Chadha* violation, or unduly impinge on Executive authority. And if it ever came to pass that Presidents did view the veto as their only option, they often would not exercise it. If they took the Task Force Report's either/or resolution to heart, they often would swallow their constitutional objections and sign the bill without objection, after which the only options would be unannounced nonenforcement of the dubious provisions or enforcement of unconstitutional laws. That result would, in our judgment, be perverse, depriving the public and the Congress of useful information for no good purpose.

There's yet another problem with this sign-it-or-veto-it view: In many such cases, the President's view, reflected in signing statements, is not that entire statutory provisions are facially unconstitutional, but merely that the laws might be unconstitutional in some future hypothetical applications. Does even that possibility of some future constitutional concern require a veto? And if not, would the President later be required to enforce the law in an unconstitutional manner?

In sum, we think longstanding practice represents the better view. As Walter Dellinger put the point in a [July 31, 2006] Op-ED in the *New York Times*:

> When a bill with a thousand provisions includes one that is unconstitutional, the Constitution does not force the president to choose between two starkly unpalatable options: veto the entire bill or enforce an unconstitutional provision. A signing statement that announces the president's intention to disregard the invalid provision offers a valuable, and lawful, alternative.

(As explained above, however, we do believe that before resorting to non-enforcement, the President should explore alternatives less threatening to the lawmaking process, including corrections to legislation before passage, interpreting genuinely ambiguous provisions to avoid constitutional problems, and consideration of the possibility of a veto and reenactment without the unconstitutional provision.)

"The president can, in effect, rewrite the statute without the possibility of either congressional or judicial oversight. . . . In this regard, the president is not above the law; he is the law."

The President Should Not Use Signing Statements

Robert Justin Lipkin

Robert Justin Lipkin is a professor at Widener University School of Law and the author of Constitutional Revolutions: Pragmatism and the Role of Judicial Review in American Constitutionalism. *In the following viewpoint, he argues that the U.S. government is built around a system of checks and balances. He says that the George W. Bush Administration has used signing statements to subvert those checks and balances, essentially rewriting laws without legislative or judicial review. Lipkin maintains the only remedy is a constitutional amendment banning signing statements. However, he notes that such an amendment is very unlikely.*

Robert Justin Lipkin, "The First State Celebrates Constitution Day 2008: Signing Statements and Constitutional Dictatorship," *Widener Law*, 2008. Reproduced by permission.

As you read, consider the following questions:

1. Which president initiated signing statements, according to Robert Justin Lipkin?

2. At the time Lipkin was writing, how many legislative provisions had President George W. Bush challenged through signing statements?

3. What catch-22 does Congress face in writing a law to make signing statements illegal, according to Lipkin?

Legend has it that when General George Washington learned of the plan to offer him the chance to become the first American king, he bristled at the idea and replied disdainfully: "I did not spend seven years waging war against George III only to become George I." Apocryphal or not, one thing is perfectly clear. Washington stands alone as the exemplar of a revolutionary leader surrendering power that he could have easily retained. Rather than assume the throne, Washington warned his fellow revolutionaries against creating an American monarchy.

Checks and Balances

Five years later [1787], at the Constitutional Convention, the Framers heeded Washington's admonition by creating a government based on the separation of federal powers. In this system, the powers of the three co-equal branches of government are designed to check and balance each other. The goal of this design was to prevent any branch from arrogating [taking] to itself more than its constitutionally authorized share of power.

Here's how American lawmaking operates. Congress passes a bill and the president signs or vetoes it. If the bill is signed and challenged, the Supreme Court may strike it down. If the bill is vetoed, Congress may override the veto, but only when a supermajority of congresspersons so desire. This conception

Obama's First Signing Statement

President [Barack] Obama issued his first signing statement last week [March 11, 2009]. While approving the
$410 billion omnibus appropriations bill, he reserved the
right to reinterpret, evade, or ignore a number of the
bill's provisions. To some conservatives, that smelled like
vindication; and some liberals found it fishy. Who's right?
Both, to some extent.

Gene Healy, "Obama's First Signing Statement,"
Cato Liberty, March 19, 2009. www.cato-at-liberty.org.

of the presidential role, as an executive not a lawmaker, com-
ports with the Framers' vision of a limited government where
no one branch or person is above the law.

Signing statements complicate this familiar picture of
American lawmaking. Initiated by President James Monroe, a
signing statement serves to alert the public and the executive
branch of how the president interprets a law as well as how he
wants the law administered. In the contemporary context of
the administrative state, such instruction may be critical to
the execution of the law. Nevertheless, signing statements have
been used sparingly. From James Monroe through the administration of Bill Clinton, presidents have used signing statements approximately 600 times.

Then came President George W. Bush, who has used signing statements as a virtual line-item veto, a device through
which the president vetoes particular provisions of a bill that
he has signed into law. Because the Supreme Court appropriately has held the line-item veto unconstitutional, President
Bush has no recourse to it. However, he has gotten around the
Supreme Court's decision by utilizing signing statements. Of

course, a signing statement is not identical to a line-item veto. The former preserves the provision for a later president to reinterpret. The line-item veto excises the provision entirely. But if available, both can be used to nullify the current legal effect of a statutory provision.

A signing statement permits the president to sign a bill while at the same time expressing his intention not to enforce certain of the bill's provisions. In the seven-plus years of his presidency [since 2001], President Bush has used signing statements to challenge the constitutionality of 1,100 provisions, almost double the number of times that all presidents combined have used signing statements.

Rewriting Statutes

Here is an example of a [March 2006] Bush signing statement, one pertaining to the reauthorization of the Patriot Act. The reauthorized bill expanded the president's powers, but it also created congressional oversight ostensibly to prevent the president from overreaching. This particular signing statement reads: "The executive branch shall construe provisions of [the Act] that call for furnishing information to entities [Congress] outside the executive branch ... in a manner consistent with the President's constitutional authority to supervise the unitary executive branch and to withhold information the disclosure of which would impair foreign relations, national security, the deliberative process of the Executive, or the performance of the Executive's constitutional duties." As Pulitzer Prize journalist, Charlie Savage, states in his book, *Takeover: The Return of the Imperial Presidency and the Subversion of American Democracy* [2007], "Bush was claiming that only parts of the bill that expanded his power were constitutional, essentially nullifying the parts of the bill that check those new powers." Congressional oversight was the victim of this signing statement and with it any check on presidential power.

The implications of this use of signing statements should be clear. By claiming the authority to reject various provisions of a bill signed into law by a president, the president can, in effect, rewrite the statute without the possibility of either congressional or judicial oversight. If left to stand, the presidency becomes an unchecked power, a constitutional dictatorship. In this regard, the president is not above the law; he is the law. The principle of the separation of power, and its attendant checks and balances, are eviscerated. Furthermore, this abuse of signing statements, in effect, abandons President Washington's noble rejection of monarchical power.

Law, Amendment, or Faith

How can this abuse of signing statements be remedied? One possibility is to encourage all presidents, in good faith, to refrain from using signing statements in an abusive fashion. This would require the president to refrain from issuing signing statements designed to nullify essential provisions of a law, especially congressional and judicial oversight provisions. However, can we rely merely on good faith?

Another possibility for preventing abuse is for Congress to pass a law regulating or prohibiting signing statements. However, this throws the baby out with the bath water, and presents a separation of powers problem as well. Congress is not authorized to regulate the Executive branch by passing laws concerning what a president is permitted to do when signing a bill into law.

There is something more problematic about a congressional attempt to prevent the abuse of signing statements. In the limiting case, a congressional remedy faces a catch-22 obstacle. In signing the remedy, the president can issue a signing statement nullifying the remedy's effect. This dilemma shows how insidious the abuse of signing statements can be.

The only remaining remedy is a constitutional amendment, which would prohibit signing statements from having any legal force. Such an amendment, however, would prevent the legitimate use of signing statements. Moreover, amending the Constitution is an onerous prospect. Only twenty-seven amendments have survived the process in more than two hundred years. Perhaps encouraging good faith is the only plausible remedy available. However, good faith is a rather slender shield against constitutional dictatorship.

> *"Congress has demonstrated that it is more than willing to employ the full weight of the rule of law pertaining to armed conflict against our enemies."*

Congress Should Expand Executive Powers to Detain and Try Suspects

Jeffrey Addicott

Jeffrey Addicott is a professor at St. Mary's University School of Law and was formerly a Lieutenant Colonel in the U.S. Army Judge Advocate General's Corps. In the following viewpoint, he argues that, given the War on Terror, Congress did the right thing in granting the executive branch broad powers in the Military Commissions Act (MCA) of 2006. The MCA restricted the rights of enemy combatants to habeas corpus, allowed hearsay to be used against them, and established other guidelines that Addicott says are both necessary and within the framework of the Geneva Conventions.

Jeffrey Addicott, "The Military Commissions Act: Congress Commits to the War on Terror," *JURIST*, October 9, 2006. Reproduced by permission.

As you read, consider the following questions:

1. What does Jeffrey Addicott refer to as an "advance signal" that Congress was willing to address the legal issues presented by the War on Terror?

2. According to Addicott, should evidence obtained without a search warrant be admissible before the military commissions?

3. Why does Addicott believe the U.S. Supreme Court will not strike down the MCA provisions as unconstitutional?

With the passage of the Military Commissions Act of 2006 (MCA), Congress has firmly committed itself to the view that the nation is at war and that the legislative branch of government has a significant role to play in a variety of legal issues associated with the "enemy combatants"— both legal and illegal—that seek to do great physical harm to the United States and its allies. While the Detainee Treatment Act of 2005 provided an advanced signal that Congress was at last willing to get involved in a limited manner in some of the thorny legal aspects of the War on Terror, the MCA represents a major Congressional shift in scope. In short, the MCA is a resounding statutory broadside that impacts forcefully and with great effect across the entire legal landscape.

Congress Enters the War on Terror

Above all, the MCA has certainly washed away all doubt regarding Congress' willingness to characterize the War on Terror as a real global war against real enemies who desire to murder and terrorize. Accordingly, Congress has demonstrated that it is more than willing to employ the full weight of the rule of law pertaining to armed conflict against our enemies. Prompted by the Supreme Court's holding in *Hamdan v.*

Rumsfeld,[1] an energized Congress understood that they could no longer remain on the sidelines in the War on Terror. Congress established the creation of military commissions, affirming quite satisfactorily that the MCA is consistent with the requirements of Common Article 3 of the Geneva Conventions[2]—the military commissions so established constitute a "regularly constituted court," affording all the necessary "judicial guarantees which are recognized as indispensable by civilized peoples."

Not only does the MCA provide crystal clear guidance in the context of the establishment and operation of military commissions to try "any alien unlawful enemy combatant" (al-Qa'eda and al-Qa'eda-styled Islamic terrorists) it provides concrete statutory definitions concerning a wide variety of terms that have been previously hotly debated. The MCA also clearly places a large legal "seal of approval" on many of the initiatives taken by the [George W.] Bush Administration in the War on Terror. For instance, the MCA defines "unlawful enemy combatants" in precise language while recognizing in the same breath the lawful functioning of the Combatant Status Review Tribunal for enemy combatant determination set up by the Department of Defense in response to the 2004 *Hamdi v. Rumsfeld* ruling:

(i) a person who has engaged in hostilities or who has purposefully and materially supported hostilities against the United States or its co-belligerents who is not a lawful enemy combatant (including a person who is part of the Taliban, al Qaeda, or associated forces); or

(ii) a person who, before, on, or after the date of the enactment of the Military Commissions Act of 2006, has been determined to be an unlawful enemy combatant by a Com-

1. In *Hamdan v. Rumsfeld*, 2006, the Supreme Court ruled that military commissions established by the George W. Bush Administration violated the Geneva Conventions governing conduct in war.
2. The Geneva Conventions are international laws governing the conduct of war.

batant Status Review Tribunal or another competent tribunal established under the authority of the President or the Secretary of Defense.

Wartime Law

The MCA also lists in detail the criminal offenses that fall within the jurisdiction of the military commission. Apart from the traditional list of war crimes the MCA appropriately includes "conspiracy" and "providing material support for terrorism.". . . In addition, reaffirming the fact that the United States is in a state of hostilities, the MCA addresses the matter of streamlining the process for dealing with the large number of petitions filed by lawyers on behalf [of] enemy combatants in the federal court system. Again, if one recognizes the government's premise that the nation is at war and the laws of war apply, then the MCA properly deals with restricting habeas corpus[3] and providing for other limitations on the jurisdiction of civilian courts.

In the sphere of authorizing trial by military commission, the Congress wisely allows for the military commission to operate in the traditional manner of all previous military commissions (hundreds were tried by military commissions in World War II, some were even U.S. citizens) and consider, for example, hearsay evidence and information gathered without a search warrant. The MCA holds that "[e]vidence shall be admissible if the military judge determines that the evidence would have probative value to a reasonable person" and "[e]vidence shall not be excluded from trial by military commission on the grounds that the evidence was not seized pursuant to a search warrant or other authorization." While the MCA correctly excludes all statements obtained by use of torture, the MCA also tackles the hard question of statements taken from an illegal enemy combatant where a "degree of coercion is disputed." Such statements may be admissible under strict guide-

3. Habeas corpus is the right of the imprisoned to a trial.

lines depending on when they were obtained. Statements obtained before the enactment of Detainee Treatment Act [in 2005] "in which the degree of coercion is disputed may be admitted only if the military judge finds that (1) the totality of the circumstances renders the statement reliable and possessing sufficient probative value; and (2) the interests of justice would best be served by admission of the statement into evidence." Statements obtained after enactment of Detainee Treatment Act in which the degree of coercion is disputed may be admitted only if the military judge finds that in addition to (1) and (2) above, "(3) the interrogation methods used to obtain the statement do not amount to cruel, inhuman, or degrading treatment."

Common Sense Standards

Ironically, some view the common sense evidentiary provisions in the MCA as a violation of Common Article 3's requirement that the accused be afforded all the necessary "guarantees . . . recognized as indispensable by civilized peoples." Such ethnocentric views are quickly dispelled when one considers the day-to-day activity of most modern European criminal courts where hearsay is regularly considered and far different legal avenues regarding the introduction of evidence are regularly employed. Even the International Criminal Court allows hearsay. In fact, earlier calls by some (uniformed judge advocates who should have known better) that a military commission should include the same due process standards that American soldiers enjoy at a military courts martial under the Uniformed Code of Military Justice were wisely disregarded by Congress. Obviously, these "relaxed" provisions in the MCA are necessary due to the exigencies of war—witnesses and victims may be dead, investigators are not able to get to the crime scene, etc.

As various legal challenges to portions of the MCA make their way through the lower courts, e.g., the MCA revokes all

U.S. court's jurisdiction to hear habeas corpus petitions by alien enemy combatants in U.S. custody, it is highly doubtful that the Supreme Court will strike down very much of the MCA as unconstitutional. Indeed, in time of war the Court has traditionally been most reluctant to intervene in matters of national security, particularly when the executive and legislative branches have joined together in such a seamless fashion.

In summary, Congress has sat on the sidelines in the War on Terror for far too long. While rational people understand that the unique threat of al-Qa'eda-styled terrorism can only be addressed by employing the laws established for armed conflict, it is equally true that said laws of war need to be updated to encompass the new paradigm. For over five years, Congress has simply watched as the executive branch, with occasional mandates from the judicial branch, crafted and implemented an emerging rule of law. It is extremely supportive of the rule of law and vital to the issue of legitimacy that the legislative branch of our government has finally joined the process.

> "The courts, including the Supreme Court, have admittedly been more effective than Congress in restraining executive excesses, but both have been too slow."

Congress Should Limit Executive Powers to Detain and Try Suspects

Arlen Specter

Arlen Specter is a Democratic U.S. Senator from Pennsylvania. In the following viewpoint, he argues that Congress has been too ready to allow expansions of executive power. He notes that Congress voted to allow the unconstitutional suspension of habeas corpus rights for detainees before military commissions. The Supreme Court eventually tossed out this law, but Specter argues that more Congressional, not just Judicial, vigilance is necessary to restore the constitutional system of checks and balances.

Arlen Specter, "The Need to Roll Back Presidential Power Grabs," *The New York Review of Books*, vol. 56, May 14, 2009. Copyright © 2009 by NYREV, Inc. Reprinted with permission from *The New York Review of Books*.

As you read, consider the following questions:

1. Arlen Specter says he intends to introduce legislation mandating Supreme Court review of lower court decisions in what kinds of cases?

2. Which Supreme Court decision said that a U.S. citizen held as an enemy combatant must be given an opportunity to contest the factual basis for his detention?

3. What actions of the Barack Obama administration does Specter say are not encouraging?

In the seven and a half years since September 11 [2001], the United States has witnessed one of the greatest expansions of executive authority in its history, at the expense of the constitutionally mandated separation of powers. President [Barack] Obama, as only the third sitting senator to be elected president in American history, and the first since John F. Kennedy, may be more likely to respect the separation of powers than President [George W.] Bush was. But rather than put my faith in any president to restrain the executive branch, I intend to take several concrete steps, which I hope the new president will support.

Rebalancing the Executive

First, I intend to introduce legislation that will mandate Supreme Court review of lower court decisions in suits brought by the ACLU[1] and others that challenge the constitutionality of the warrantless wiretapping program authorized by President Bush after September 11. While the Supreme Court generally exercises discretion on whether it will review a case, there are precedents for Congress to direct Supreme Court review on constitutional issues—including the statutes forbidding flag burning and requiring Congress to abide by federal employment laws—and I will follow those.

1. The American Civil Liberties Union (ACLU) often files court cases on constitutional issues.

Second, I will reintroduce legislation to keep the courts open to suits filed against several major telephone companies that allegedly facilitated the Bush administration's warrantless wiretapping program.[2] Although Congress granted immunity to the telephone companies in July 2008, this issue may yet be successfully revisited since the courts have not yet ruled on the legality of the immunity provision. My legislation would substitute the government as defendant in place of the telephone companies. This would allow the cases to go forward, with the government footing the bill for any damages awarded.

Further, I will reintroduce my legislation from 2006 and 2007 (the "Presidential Signing Statements Act") to prohibit courts from relying on, or deferring to, presidential signing statements when determining the meaning of any Act of Congress. These statements, sometimes issued when the president signs a bill into law, have too often been used to undermine congressional intent. Earlier versions of my legislation went nowhere because of the obvious impossibility of obtaining two-thirds majorities in each house to override an expected veto by President Bush. Nevertheless, in the new Congress, my legislation has a better chance of mustering a majority vote and being signed into law by President Obama.

To understand why these steps are so important, one must appreciate an imbalance in our "checks and balances" that has become increasingly evident in recent years. I witnessed first-hand, during many of the battles over administration policy since September 11, how difficult it can be for Congress and the courts to rally their members against an overzealous executive. . . .

Restore Habeas Corpus

The courts, including the Supreme Court, have admittedly been more effective than Congress in restraining executive ex-cesses, but both have been too slow. This failure is exemplified

2. The National Security Agency (NSA) tapped phones without warrants during the George W. Bush administration.

by the judicial and legislative efforts to address the administration's treatment of detainees in the war on terror.

In *Hamdi v. Rumsfeld*, decided on June 28, 2004, nearly three years after September 11, the Supreme Court ruled that a United States citizen being held as an enemy combatant must be given an opportunity to contest the factual basis for his detention before a neutral magistrate. In a stern rebuke of executive overreaching, Justice Sandra Day O'Connor's opinion declared, "We have long since made clear that a state of war is not a blank check for the President when it comes to the rights of the Nation's citizens." The same day, the Court held in *Rasul v. Bush* that detainees at Guantánamo Bay were entitled to challenge their detention by filing habeas corpus petitions—the time-honored legal action used to contest the basis for government confinement.[3] Two years later, on June 29, 2006, the Court announced in *Hamdan v. Rumsfeld* that the president could not conduct military commission trials under procedures that had not been authorized by Congress and that failed to satisfy the obligations of the Geneva Conventions' Common Article III[4] and the Uniform Code of Military Justice.

Instead of fully accepting these decisions, however, Congress responded with the Detainee Treatment Act and the Military Commissions Act of 2006, both of which eliminated detainees' right to habeas corpus review on grounds that foreign terrorist suspects did not have the same rights as others in US custody.

During debate on the Military Commissions Act, I offered an amendment that would have guaranteed habeas corpus for detainees. In the face of sharp criticism from my own party, I argued that I was not speaking "in favor of enemy combatants." Rather, I was "trying to establish . . . a course of judicial procedure" to determine whether the accused were in fact en-

3. Habeas corpus refers to the right of those imprisoned to receive a trial.
4. The Geneva Conventions are international laws governing the conduct of war.

emy combatants. I pointed out that my fight to preserve habeas rights was, in essence, a struggle to defend "the jurisdiction of the federal courts to maintain the rule of law." I concluded with a plea for the Senate not to deny "the habeas corpus right which would take us back some 900 years and deny the fundamental principle of the Magna Carta imposed on King John at Runnymede."[5]Despite these entreaties, my amendment narrowly lost on a 48–51 vote.

I had lost the battle, but was not prepared to surrender. On January 18, 2007, Attorney General [Alberto] Gonzales testified before the Judiciary Committee and argued that proposals to restore habeas corpus, such as a bill Senator [Patrick] Leahy and I had introduced, were "ill-advised and frankly defy common sense." I was astounded at his claim that "there is no express grant of habeas in the Constitution." I asked him:

> The constitution says you can't take it away except in case of rebellion or invasion. Doesn't that mean you have the right of habeas corpus unless there is an invasion or rebellion?

He replied,

> The constitution does not say every individual in the United States or every citizen is hereby granted or assured the right to habeas. . . . It simply says the right of habeas corpus shall not be suspended.

I protested, "You may be treading on your interdiction and violating common sense, Mr. Attorney General."

That September, I made a second attempt to restore habeas corpus jurisdiction with an amendment to the Defense Department's authorization bill. This time, a majority of senators voted for it, including seven Republicans. Unfortunately,

---

5. In the Magna Carta, a legal charter issued in 1215, King John of England granted numerous rights to his subjects.

The Supreme Court Opinion in *Hamdi v. Rumsfeld*

We have long since made clear that a state of war is not a blank check for the President when it comes to the rights of the Nation's citizens. . . . Whatever power the United States Constitution envisions for the Executive in its exchanges with other nations or with enemy organizations in times of conflict, it most assuredly envisions a role for all three branches when individual liberties are at stake. . . . Likewise, we have made clear that, unless Congress acts to suspend it, the Great Writ of habeas corpus allows the Judicial Branch to play a necessary role in maintaining this delicate balance of governance, serving as an important judicial check on the Executive's discretion in the realm of detentions. . . . Thus, while we do not question that our due process assessment must pay keen attention to the particular burdens faced by the Executive in the context of military action, it would turn our system of checks and balances on its head to suggest that a citizen could not make his way to court with a challenge to the factual basis for his detention by his government, simply because the Executive opposes making available such a challenge. Absent suspension of the writ by Congress, a citizen detained as an enemy combatant is entitled to this process. . . .

Sandra Day O'Connor,
Hamdi v. Rumsfeld: Opinion of O'Connor, 2004.
www.law.cornell.edu.

the 56-43 majority was insufficient because, in the face of a filibuster threat, Senate procedure required sixty votes to pass. Ironically, a procedure intended to protect Senate minorities had become a shield for the executive branch.

The Court Acts Where Congress Will Not

Thus, yet again, it was left to the Supreme Court to beat back the encroachment of executive power, which it finally did on June 12, 2008. In *Boumediene v. Bush*, the Court held that detainees held at Guantánamo Bay "are entitled to the privilege of habeas corpus to challenge the legality of their detention." The Court said that the Combatant Status Review Tribunals established by the Defense Department in 2004, following the *Hamdi* and *Rasul* decisions, and the limited procedural review permitted before the D.C. Circuit were not an adequate and effective substitute for habeas corpus. Because the administration had failed to provide an adequate substitute for habeas corpus, the Court held that the Military Commissions Act had effected "an unconstitutional suspension of the writ."

As satisfying as it was to be vindicated, I was frustrated that Congress had left the task of reining in the executive to slow-paced and incomplete judicial review. While the *Boumediene* decision ensured habeas rights for detainees, it took seven years; and even then the Court almost failed to take on the case. All along, the Court's rulings were piecemeal and avoided taking strong stands on controversial constitutional questions. The result was a protracted process that delayed justice for detainees and left important areas of constitutional law murky.

Indeed, the Supreme Court actually denied Boumediene's initial petition for review on April 2, 2007. Then, on June 29, in a highly unusual move, the Court reconsidered and agreed to hear the case. The justices gave no reason for the reversal, but some speculate that they were moved by intervening disclosures concerning the military commissions. In particular, a military officer and lawyer who had been involved in overseeing the tribunals said that the process was flawed and that prosecutors had been pressured to label detainees as enemy combatants.

As much time as it took in these cases, at least the Supreme Court, in 2008, eventually ruled on the merits in *Boumediene*. The same cannot be said for Supreme Court review, or even substantive appellate review, of President Bush's warrantless wiretapping program. Thus far, only individual judges in the district courts of Michigan and California have been willing to take a strong stand on the Terrorist Surveillance Program.

Like many in the legislature, the courts are reluctant to act. They do not want the responsibility, perhaps because of a longstanding reluctance on the part of the Supreme Court to challenge the executive in military policies. Only after significant time has passed, and it is relatively safe, do they finally consider such issues on the merits. I have proposed legislation to require expedited review of certain important cases, including the challenges by civil liberties organizations and other plaintiffs to the Terrorist Surveillance Program, and I will do so again in the new Congress. . . .

Congress Must Take Responsibility

These experiences have crystallized for me the need for Congress and the courts to reassert themselves in our system of checks and balances. The bills I have outlined are important steps in that process. Equally important is vigorous congressional oversight of the executive branch. This oversight must extend well beyond the problems of national security, especially as we cede more and more authority over our economy to government officials.

As for curbing executive branch excesses from within, I hope President Obama lives up to his campaign promise of change. His recent signing statements[6] have not been encouraging. Adding to the feeling of dèjá vu is *The Washington*

---

6. Signing statements are presidential statements issued when a bill is signed, sometimes declaring parts of the bill unconstitutional or unenforceable. George W. Bush used them frequently; President Barack Obama issued several before this viewpoint was written in April 2009.

Post's report that the new administration has reasserted the "state secrets"[7] privilege to block lawsuits challenging controversial policies like warrantless wiretapping: "Obama has not only maintained the Bush administration approach, but [in one such case] the dispute has intensified." Government lawyers are now asserting that the US Circuit Court in San Francisco, which is hearing the case, lacks authority to compel disclosure of secret documents, and are "warning" that the government, might "spirit away" the material before the court can release it to the litigants. I doubt that the Democratic majority, which was so eager to decry expansions of executive authority under President Bush, will still be as interested in the problem with a Democratic president in office. I will continue the fight whatever happens.

---

7. The state secrets privilege allows the government to refuse to divulge information to a court in cases where national security is at issue.

Periodical Bibliography

The following articles have been selected to supplement the diverse views presented in this chapter.

Jack M. Balkin — "Who's Afraid of Presidential Signing Statements?" *Balkinization*, January 17, 2006. http://balkin.blogspot.com.

Adam Cohen — "Congress, the Constitution and War: The Limits on Presidential Power," *New York Times*, January 29, 2007. www.nytimes.com.

John W. Dean — "The Problem with Presidential Signing Statements: Their Use and Misuse by the Bush Administration," *FindLaw*, January 13, 2006. http://writ.new.findlaw.com.

Tim Dickinson — "Investigating Bush," *Rolling Stone*, April 10, 2008. www.rollingstone.com.

Jeffrey M. Jones — "Americans Divided on Investigating Bush-Era Interrogations," www.gallup.com, September 4, 2009.

David Kaye and Robert Alt — "Dust-Up: Torture and the CIA: Investigate White House Higher-Ups?" Heritage Foundation Web site, August 28, 2009. www.heritage.org.

Charlie Savage — "Obama Undercuts Whistle-Blowers, Senator Says," *New York Times*, March 16, 2009. www.nytimes.com.

USA Today — "Our View on 'Truth Commission': Investigate Bush? U.S. Has Bigger Woes to Worry About," February 17, 2009. www.usatoday.com.

Troy Vettese — "How Many Other Times Has Congress Tried to Limit Presidential Power in Foreign Affairs?" *History News Network*, March 5, 2007. http://hnn.us.

Washington Post — "Mr. Obama Punts . . . ," September 27, 2009. www.washingtonpost.com.

Is the President Bound by International Law?

Chapter Preface

The International Criminal Court (ICC) is a tribunal that prosecutes individuals for war crimes and crimes against humanity. It is designed to investigate violations of international law in situations where national courts are unable or unwilling to do so. Since the court was established in 2002, it has investigated four instances of human rights violations, including war crimes and genocide in Darfur and in Northern Uganda.

More than 100 countries have signed on to the ICC. The United States, however, is not among them, and it does not officially recognize the ICC's jurisdiction. America has been wary of the court because the court's purpose is to ensure that "Any soldier, or combatant, who commits . . . atrocities, even under the direction of his superior, is personally and individually culpable for them." Thus, American soldiers and higher-ups who killed civilians or participated in acts of torture or abuse, "could be prosecuted for such abominations," according to Makau Mutua, writing in the Nairobi paper, *Daily Nation*, on January 11, 2004. Thomas P. Kilgannon, writing on the conservative Web site HumanEvents.com on February 10, 2009, agreed that this was the major problem with the court—it might lead to prosecutions of American officials and soldiers for such actions as abusing prisoners at Abu Ghraib prison in Iraq.

Though Matua and Kilgannon agree on why America has stayed out of the court, they differ greatly on whether this is a good decision. Matua calls U.S. efforts to weaken the court "sickening" and argues that American officials who commit human rights violations should have to answer to international law for their actions. Kilgannon, on the other hand, argues that U.S. citizens should not be prosecuted for what he believes are "actions taken to protect U.S. interests," and denigrates the ICC for not providing American citizens with the protection of the U.S. Constitution and U.S. laws.

The debate points to a basic difference in perspective: Should the United States and the U.S. president be accountable for their actions to the rest of the world? Or is the United States accountable only to its own people and its own laws? The authors of the following viewpoints further explore whether international obligations and institutions can, or should, put limits on the power of the United States and of its president.

> "Although the Constitution does not spe-
> cifically mention the power to suspend
> or terminate treaties, these authorities
> have been understood by the courts and
> long executive branch practice as be-
> longing solely to the President."

The President Is Not Bound by the Geneva Conventions in Dealing with Terrorists

Jay Bybee

Jay Bybee served in the Office of Legal Counsel in the George W. Bush administration, and he is now a federal U.S. Appeals Court judge. In the following viewpoint, he argues that the Geneva Conventions govern war between states, and that they therefore do not apply to a terrorist organization such as al Qaeda. He further argues that the Taliban government of Afghanistan was illegitimate and, therefore, not subject to the Geneva Conventions. Finally, Bybee contends that the president, as commander-in-chief, has the power to suspend portions of treaties, such as Geneva protection of prisoners, in some circumstances.

Jay Bybee, "Memorandum for Alberto R. Gonzales, Counsel to the President, and William J. Haynes II, General Counsel of the Department of Defense, Re: Application of Treaties and Laws to al Qaeda and Taliban Detainees," *Washington Post Online*, January 22, 2002.

As you read, consider the following questions:

1. What does Convention III of the Geneva Conventions regulate, according to the author?

2. When did Afghanistan become a party to the Geneva Conventions?

3. What two reasons does Jay Bybee provide for believing that the president could exercise the authority to suspend the Geneva Conventions in regard to the Taliban in Afghanistan?

You[1] have asked for our Office's views[2] concerning the effect of international treaties and federal laws on the treatment of individuals detained by the U.S. Armed Forces during the conflict in Afghanistan. In particular, you have asked whether certain treaties forming part of the laws of armed conflict apply to the conditions of detention and the procedures for trial of members of al Qaeda [terrorist group responsible for September 11, 2001, attacks] and the Taliban militia [political military faction in Afghanistan]. We conclude that these treaties do not protect members of the al Qaeda organization, which as a non-State actor cannot be a party to the international agreements governing war. We further conclude that that President has sufficient grounds to find that these treaties do not protect members of the Taliban militia. This memorandum expresses no view as to whether the President should decide, as a matter of policy, that the U.S. Armed Forces should adhere to the standards of conduct in those treaties with respect to the treatment of prisoners....

1. This viewpoint was originally an internal government memo addressed to Alberto R. Gonzales, counsel to the President George W. Bush, and William J. Haynes II, general counsel of the Department of Defense.
2. That is, the views of the Office of Legal Counsel, which provides legal advice to the president.

Grave Breaches of the Geneva Conventions

The Geneva Conventions of 1949 remain the agreements to which more states have become parties than any other concerning the laws of war. Convention I deals with the treatment of wounded and sick in armed forces in the field; Convention II addresses treatment of the wounded, sick, and shipwrecked in armed forces at sea; Convention III regulates treatment of POWs [Prisoners of War]; Convention IV addresses the treatment of citizens.

The Geneva Conventions, like treaties generally, structure legal relationships between nation-States, not between nation-States and private, transnational or subnational groups or organizations. Article 2, which is common to all four Geneva Conventions, makes the application of the Conventions to relations between state parties clear. It states that: "the present Convention shall apply to all cases of declared war or of any other armed conflict *which may arise between two or more of the High Contracting Parties*, even if the state of war is not recognized by one of them." Similarly, it states that "[t]he Convention shall also apply to all cases of partial or total occupation of the territory of a High Contracting Party, even if the said occupation meets with no armed resistance."

As noted above, Section 2441(c)(1) criminalizes "grave breaches" of the Convention. Each of the Four Geneva Conventions has a similar definition of "grave breaches." Geneva Convention III defines a grave breach as:

> wilful killing, torture or inhuman treatment, including biological experiments, wilfully causing great suffering or serious injury to body or health, compelling a prisoner of war to serve in the forces of the hostile Power, or wilfully depriving a prisoner of war of the rights of fair and regular trial prescribed in this Convention.

Given the specific definition of "grave breaches," it bears noting that not *all* breaches of the Geneva Conventions are criminalized.... Failure to follow some of the regulations regarding the treatment of POWs, such as difficulty in meeting all of the conditions set forth for POW camp conditions, does not constitute a grave breach.... Only by causing great suffering or serious bodily injury to POWs, killing or torturing them, depriving them of access to a fair trial, or forcing them to serve in the Armed Forces, could the United States actually commit a grave breach....

Common Article 3 of the Geneva Conventions

Common article 3 [of the Geneva Conventions] may require the United States, as a High Contracting Party, to follow certain rules even if other parties to the conflict are not parties to the Conventions. On the other hand, article 3 requires State parties to follow only certain minimum standards of treatment toward prisoners, civilians, or the sick and wounded—standards that are much less onerous and less detailed than those spelled out in the Conventions as a whole....

Common article 3's text provides substantial reason to think that it refers specifically to a condition of civil war, or a large-scale armed conflict between a State and an armed movement within its own territory. First, the text of the provision refers specifically to an armed conflict that a) is not of an international character, and b) occurs in the territory of a state party to the Convention. It does not sweep in all armed conflicts, nor does it address a gap left by common article 2 for international armed conflicts that involve non-state entities (such as an international terrorist organization) as parties to the conflict. Further, common article 3 addresses only non-international conflicts that occur within the territory of a single state party, again, like a civil war. This provision would not reach an armed conflict in which one of the parties operated from multiple bases in several different states....

Geneva Does Not Apply to al Qaeda

We conclude that Geneva III does not apply to the al Qaeda terrorist organization. Therefore, neither the detention nor trial of al Qaeda fighters is subject to Geneva III. . . . Three reasons, examined in detail below, support this conclusion. First, al Qaeda is not a State and thus cannot receive the benefits of a State party to the Conventions. Second, al Qaeda members fail to satisfy the eligibility requirements for treatment as POWs under Geneva Convention III. Third, the nature of the conflict precludes application of common article 3 of the Geneva Conventions.

Geneva III does not apply to a non-State actor such as the al Qaeda terrorist organization. Al Qaeda is not a State. It is a non-governmental terrorist organization composed of members from many nations, with ongoing operations in dozens of nations. Non-governmental organizations cannot be parties to any of the international agreements here governing the laws of war. Common article 2, which triggers the Geneva Convention provisions regulating detention conditions and procedures for trial of POWs, is limited to cases of declared war or armed conflict "between two or more of the High Contracting Parties." Al Qaeda is not a High Contracting Party. As a result, the U.S. military's treatment of al Qaeda members is not governed by the bulk of the Geneva Conventions, specifically those provisions concerning POWs. . . .

Second, al Qaeda members fail to satisfy the eligibility requirements for treatment as POWs under Geneva Convention III. . . .

Al Qaeda is not the "armed forces," volunteer forces, or militia of a state party that is a party to the conflict, as defined in article 4(A)(1). . . . They cannot qualify as volunteer force, militia, or organized resistance force under article 4(A)(2). That article requires that militia or volunteers fulfill four conditions: command by responsible individuals, wearing insignia, carrying arms openly, and obeying the laws of war.

Al Qaeda members have clearly demonstrated that they will not follow these basic requirements of lawful warfare. They have attacked purely civilian targets of no military value; they refused to wear uniform or insignia or carry arms openly, but instead hijacked civilian airliners, took hostages, and killed them; and they themselves do not obey the laws of war concerning the protection of the lives of civilians or the means of legitimate combat. . . .

Third, the nature of the conflict precludes application of common article 3 of the Geneva Conventions. . . . The Geneva Conventions were intended to cover either: a) traditional wars between state parties to the Conventions (article 2), b) or non-international civil wars (article 3). Our conflict with al Qaeda does not fit into either category. It is not an international war between nation-States because al Qaeda is not a State. Nor is this conflict a civil war under article 3, because it *is* a conflict of "an international character." Al Qaeda operates in many countries and carried out a massive international attack on the United States on September 11, 2001. Therefore, the military's treatment of al Qaeda members is not limited . . . by common article 3. . . .

Suspending the Geneva Conventions

Whether the Geneva Conventions apply to the detention and trial of members of the Taliban militia presents a more difficult legal question.[3] Afghanistan has been a party to all four Geneva Conventions since September 1956. Some might argue that this requires application of the Geneva Conventions to the present conflict with respect to the Taliban militia, which would then trigger the WCA.[4] Nonetheless, we conclude that the President has more than ample grounds to find that our treaty obligations under Geneva III toward Afghanistan were suspended during the period of the conflict. Under Article II

3. The Taliban is an Afghan military and political faction. They controlled Afghanistan when the U.S. invaded that country in 2001.
4. The WCA, or War Crimes Act, incorporates the Geneva Conventions into U.S. law.

The Geneva Conventions and al Qaeda Terrorists

The Geneva Conventions basically hold that soldiers who conduct themselves in such a way as to protect innocent noncombatants . . . deserve to be treated humanely when they are captured by enemy forces.

In other words, those who fight by the rules are protected by the Conventions when they become prisoners of war. It follows that those who don't play by the rules are not covered. Obviously, al Qaeda terrorists are dedicated to behaving in a way that is the exact opposite of what was intended. They deliberately target innocent noncombatants; they dress like noncombatants so they can hide among the innocent; and they deliberately place themselves among innocent noncombatants so as to maximize casualties among them when civilized forces attack.

Why, then, would anyone ever suggest that al Qaeda terrorists should be protected by the Geneva Convention.

Engram, "The Geneva Convention and al Qaeda Terrorists," Back Talk, March 18, 2009. http://engram-backtalk.blogspot.com.

of the Constitution, the President has the unilateral power to suspend whole treaties or parts of them at his discretion. In this part, we describe the President's constitutional power and discuss the grounds upon which he can justify the exercise of that power.

There are several grounds [on] which . . . the President could exercise that authority here. First, the weight of informed opinion indicates that, for the period in question, Afghanistan was a "failed State" whose territory had been largely held by a violent militia or faction rather than by a government. As a failed state, Afghanistan did not have an operating government nor was it capable of fulfilling its international obligations. Therefore, the United States could decide to partially suspend any obligations that the United States might have under Geneva III towards the Taliban militia. Second, there appears to be developing evidence that the Taliban leadership had become closely intertwined with, if not utterly dependent upon, al Qaeda. This would have rendered the Taliban more akin to a terrorist organization that used force not to administer a government, but for terrorist purposes. The President could decide that no treaty obligations were owed to such a force.

Article II of the Constitution makes clear that the President is vested with all of the federal executive power, that he "shall be Commander in Chief." . . .

On the few occasions where it has addressed the question, the Supreme Court has lent its approval to the executive branch's broad powers in the field of foreign affairs. Responsibility for the conduct of foreign affairs and for protecting national security are, as the Supreme Court has observed, "'central Presidential domains.'" The President's constitutional primacy flows from both his unique position in the constitutional structure and from the specific grants of authority in Article II making the President the Chief Executive of the Nation and the Commander in Chief. . . .

In light of these principles, any unenumerated executive power, especially one relating to foreign affairs, must be construed as within the control of the President. Although the Constitution does not specifically mention the power to suspend or terminate treaties, these authorities have been understood by the courts and long executive branch practice as belonging solely to the President. The treaty power is fundamentally an executive power established in Article II of the Constitution, and power over treaty matters post-ratification are within the President's plenary authority. . . .

Exercising this constitutional authority, the President can decide to suspend temporarily our obligations under Geneva III toward Afghanistan. Other Presidents have partially suspended treaties, and have suspended the obligations of multilateral agreements with regard to one of the state parties. The President could also determine that relations under the Geneva Conventions with Afghanistan should be restored once an Afghan government that is willing and able to execute the country's treaty obligations is securely established.

"The President never possesses the uni-
lateral authority to violate a treaty; he
must always obtain congressional ap-
proval."

The President Is Bound
by the Geneva Conventions
in Wartime

Derek Jinks and David Sloss

Derek Jinks is associate professor of law at Arizona State Univer-
sity College of Law; David Sloss is associate professor of law at
Saint Louis University School of Law. In the following viewpoint,
they argue that the president does not have the power to violate
treaties, such as the Geneva Conventions, at will. Instead, they
argue, it is Congress that has the power to overturn treaties. If
the president alone could overturn treaties, they say, it would
violate the separation of powers, and effectively place the presi-
dent above the law.

Derek Jinks and David Sloss, "Is the President Bound by the Geneva Conventions?" *Cornell Law Review*, vol. 90, November 2004, pp. 97–200. Copyright © 2004 Cornell University. Reproduced by permission of the publisher and the authors.

As you read, consider the following questions:

1. According to the authors, does the George W. Bush administration believe it has a legal right to disregard the Geneva Conventions on the basis of international or domestic law?

2. Based on the oath of office, under what circumstances have presidents claimed the right to violate the law, according to the authors?

3. What is the strong version of the emergency powers thesis, according to the authors?

During wartime, the executive branch tends to accrue greater powers at the expense of its legislative and judicial counterparts. Throughout most of U.S. constitutional history, the powers accrued by the executive branch during wartime reverted back to the other branches in peacetime. This reversion did not occur, however, at the end of World War II [1939–45]. As one distinguished scholar [Edwin S. Corwin] observed, "for the first time in . . . history there [was], following a great war, no peacetime Constitution to which [the American people could] expect to return in any wholesale way, inasmuch as the Constitution of peacetime and the Constitution of wartime ha[d] become . . . very much the same Constitution." Another respected scholar [Arthur M. Schlesinger, Jr.], writing at the end of the Vietnam War [1954–75], warned that "unless the American democracy figures out how to control the Presidency in war and peace . . . our system of government will face grave troubles."

The War on Terror

Recently, in the context of the "War on Terror," President [George W.] Bush has attempted to build on precedents established during past wars to support extraordinarily broad claims of executive power. In 2002, a top legal advisor in the

Justice Department [Jay S. Bybee] told the White House that "the President enjoys complete discretion in the exercise of his Commander-in-Chief authority." Moreover, the legal advisor added, "Congress lacks authority under Article I to set the terms and conditions under which the President may exercise his authority as Commander in Chief." In short, when the President invokes his Commander-in-Chief power, he is free to take any action that he believes will promote national security, and Congress is powerless to interfere with the exercise of presidential prerogative.

The Bush Administration's sweeping claims of executive power have not gone unchallenged. In *Hamdi v. Rumsfeld* [2004], the Supreme Court held that a U.S. citizen held captive in a military prison as an alleged "enemy combatant" has a right to challenge the factual basis of his detention. In *Rasul v. Bush* [2004], the Court held that aliens imprisoned at Guantanamo Bay, Cuba ("Guantanamo") as "enemy combatants" have a right of access to U.S. courts. While *Hamdi* and *Rasul* impose significant limitations on executive power in wartime, the Court's decisions leave a number of crucial questions unanswered.

One such question is whether the President possesses the constitutional authority to violate treaties that regulate the conduct of warfare. Currently, the Bush Administration is holding approximately six hundred prisoners at Guantanamo, most of whom were captured during the armed conflict in Afghanistan. Assuming that neither the Taliban[1] nor the al Qaeda [terrorist group] detainees qualify as prisoners of war under the Geneva Convention[2] Relative to the Treatment of Prisoners of War ("POW Convention"), as the Bush Administration maintains, they are still entitled to the protections of the Geneva Convention Relative to the Protection of Civilian Persons in Time of War ("Civilian Convention"), which applies to

1. The Taliban are a political military faction in Afghanistan with ties to al-Qaeda.
2. The Geneva Conventions are international agreements governing conduct in wartime.

all "those who, at a given moment and in any manner whatsoever, find themselves, in case of a conflict or occupation, in the hands of a Party to the conflict . . . of which they are not nationals." The Bush Administration claims that it is treating the Guantanamo detainees "in a manner consistent with the principles of [the Conventions]." Even so, the Administration reserves the right to deviate from specific requirements of the Conventions "to the extent appropriate and consistent with military necessity."

The Geneva Conventions and the President

Is the President bound, in any meaningful sense, by the Geneva Conventions? Do the treaties, applicable only in a time of war, condition the exercise of the President's Commander-in-Chief power? The Bush Administration would answer both questions in the negative. As a matter of international law, it would be untenable to claim that the United States has a legal right to disregard its obligations under the Geneva Conventions. The Administration's claim, however, is primarily one of domestic, rather than international law. The "Bush position" boils down to this: even assuming that the Geneva Conventions are binding on the United States as a matter of international law, they do not bind the President as a matter of domestic law because the President has the constitutional authority to violate specific provisions of the Conventions to protect national security. . . .

Several scholars have analyzed the President's authority to terminate treaties in accordance with international law. One should recognize, however, that treaty termination and treaty violation raise distinct constitutional issues. A presidential decision to terminate a treaty in compliance with international law is generally considered consistent with the President's constitutional duty [in Article II] to "take Care that the Laws be faithfully executed." In contrast, a presidential decision to breach a treaty, in contravention of international law, may violate the President's duty under the Take Care Clause.

Scholars have also published numerous articles concerning the President's authority to violate customary international law (CIL). Treaties raise different constitutional issues, however, because the Supremacy Clause [in Article VI of the Constitution] expressly states that treaties, like statutes, are the "supreme Law of the Land." . . . Therefore, even if the President does possess the constitutional authority to violate CIL, it does not necessarily follow that the President has the constitutional authority to violate a treaty that is the supreme law of the land.

The question of whether the President is bound by the Geneva Conventions also implicates unique issues involving the President's Commander-in-Chief power. The Conventions belong to a fairly small class of treaties that regulates the conduct of warfare. Scholars have written extensively about the relationship between the President's Commander-in-Chief power and Congress's power to declare war. In addition to the Declare War Clause,[3] however, the Constitution grants Congress several other powers related to the conduct of warfare. Strikingly, there is very little commentary on the relationship between these congressional powers and the President's Commander-in-Chief power. . . . It is firmly established that Congress has the power to violate U.S. treaty obligations within the scope of Article I by enacting legislation that supersedes a particular treaty provision as a matter of domestic law. If the Geneva Conventions govern matters beyond the scope of Congress's Article I powers, however, then either the President has the constitutional authority to violate the treaties or the federal government as a whole lacks the power.

3. The Declare War Clause of the Constitution gives Congress the power to declare war.

No Presidential Power

This [viewpoint] contends that the President never possesses the unilateral authority to violate a treaty; he must always obtain congressional approval. Moreover, the courts have a meaningful role to play in enforcing treaties. . . .

Presidents and their subordinates have often claimed that the President is free to disregard (i.e., violate) statutes, treaties, and even the Constitution itself in certain emergency situations. In a recent memorandum [from 2002], Justice Department lawyers have asserted that President Bush has unlimited discretion to determine the appropriate means for interrogation of enemy combatants detained in the War on Terror. The memorandum further contends that treaties and statutes prohibiting torture—if applied to interrogation of enemy combatants—would be an unconstitutional infringement on the President's Commander-in-Chief power. . . .

Before any person can become President, he is required to take an oath to "preserve, protect and defend the Constitution of the United States." Relying in part on this oath, several Presidents have claimed a power to violate the law in situations where national survival is at stake. For example, Thomas Jefferson once wrote:

> The question you propose, whether circumstances do not sometimes occur, which make it a duty in officers of high trust, to assume authorities beyond the law, is easy of solution in principle, but sometimes embarrassing in practice. A strict observance of the written laws is doubtless one of the high duties of a good citizen, but it is not the highest. The laws of necessity, of self-preservation, of *saving our country when in danger*, are of higher obligation.

Jefferson added that "[t]o lose our country by a scrupulous adherence to written law, would be to lose the law itself, with life, liberty, and property and all those who are enjoying them with us; thus absurdly sacrificing the ends to the means." Thus, even Thomas Jefferson, who was more wary than most

Presidents of the dangers of unchecked executive power, recognized a presidential power to violate the law in order to protect and defend the nation. . . .

In sum, lawyers within the Bush Administration can cite substantial executive branch precedent in support of their claim that the President has the constitutional authority to violate federal statutes and treaties prohibiting torture of detainees held in the War on Terror. On the other hand, if the Constitution really does grant the President the authority to approve torture of detainees, it becomes difficult to identify the line that separates constitutional democracy from despotism. . . .

Emergency Powers

The central claim of those who advocate a presidential power to violate the law in emergency situations is that the President's duty to protect and defend the nation sometimes takes precedence over his duty to execute the laws. It is helpful to distinguish between a weaker and stronger version of this thesis. The strong version asserts that the President has the sole constitutional authority to decide what specific actions are necessary to defend the nation, and that any action the President deems necessary is ipso facto lawful, regardless of any contrary constitutional or statutory provision. Under the strong version, neither the legislative nor the judicial branch has the constitutional authority to question the President's judgment that a particular course of action is required for national security. Impeachment is the only remedy for abuse of presidential power.

Whereas the strong version provides a constitutional defense of broad presidential emergency powers, the weak version offers a legal realist account of interbranch behavior in emergency situations. According to this account, Presidents tend to adopt an expansive view of executive power during perceived emergencies, and the legislative and judicial branches tend to defer to executive judgments regarding the situation. Under the weak version, presidential action that contravenes the federal constitution or statutes is illegal, and the existence of an emergency does not make it legal. As a practical matter, however, executive officers are unlikely to be subjected to civil or criminal sanctions for violating the law if: (1) they were acting within the scope of a presidential order; (2) the legislative and judicial branches agree there was a genuine emergency; and (3) the relevant presidential order did not constitute a gross abuse of executive power.

The weak version of the emergency power thesis, understood as a descriptive theory of interbranch collaboration in times of crisis, has much to recommend it. Nevertheless, courts have generally rejected the strong version because of the resulting concentration of power in the executive branch. For example, in *Hamdi v. Rumsfeld*, the Supreme Court entertained a habeas[4] petition brought on behalf of Yaser Hamdi, an American citizen captured in Afghanistan during armed conflict between the United States and the Taliban. The Bush Administration claimed the authority to detain him indefinitely, "without formal charges or proceedings—unless and until it [the executive branch] makes the determination that access to counsel or further process is warranted." The Supreme Court rejected this claim of executive prerogative, stating:

> We have long since made clear that a state of war is not a blank check for the President when it comes to the rights of the Nation's citizens. Whatever power the United States Constitution envisions for the Executive . . . in times of conflict, it most assuredly envisions a role for all three branches when individual liberties are at stake.

The *Hamdi* Court insists that the judiciary plays a vital role in restraining executive power, even in wartime. This thesis is generally consistent with the original understanding of separation of powers. . . .

4. Habeas corpus is the right of the imprisoned to appear before a court.

Applying the Geneva Conventions

The Bush administration has agreed to apply the Geneva Conventions to all terrorism suspects in U.S. custody, bowing to the Supreme Court's recent rejection of policies that have imprisoned hundreds for years without trials.

The Pentagon announced yesterday [July 11, 2006] that it has called on military officials to adhere to the conventions in dealing with al-Qaeda detainees. The administration also has decided that even prisoners held by the CIA [Central Intelligence Agency] in secret prisons abroad must be treated in accordance with international standards, an interpretation that would prohibit prisoners from being subjected to harsh treatment in interrogations, several U.S. officials said.

Charles Babington and Michael Abramowitz,
"U.S. Shifts Policy on Geneva Conventions,"
Washington Post, *July 12, 2006.*
www.washingtonpost.com.

The Duty to Execute Treaties

Given that the President has a constitutional duty to "take Care that the Laws be faithfully executed," the question arises whether that duty also applies to treaties. . . . This section contends . . . that the Constitution is best interpreted to require the President to obtain congressional approval, in the form of legislation, if he wants to violate a treaty provision that is the law of the land. . . .

Under the Constitution, treaties are declared to be "the supreme Law of the Land" and the President is obligated to "take Care that the Laws be faithfully executed." As a textual matter, there are two possible interpretations of the word

"Laws" in the Take Care Clause. The first interpretation holds that the word "Laws" includes treaties. The fact that the Supremacy Clause declares treaties to be "the supreme Law of the Land" lends support to this interpretation. Under this interpretation, it would seem that the President does not have the constitutional power to violate treaties because his duty to execute the Laws includes a duty to execute treaties.

The second interpretation holds that the word "Laws" in the Take Care Clause excludes treaties. The fact that the Supremacy Clause distinguishes between "Laws of the United States" on the one hand, and "Treaties" on the other, lends support to this interpretation. Under this interpretation, the President arguably possesses the constitutional power to violate treaties because he does not have a constitutional duty to "take Care" that treaties are "faithfully executed." Although this textual argument initially appears plausible, it is ultimately untenable: Under this interpretation, the President would also have the power to violate the Constitution, because the Constitution, like treaties, is mentioned separately from "Laws" in the Supremacy Clause, but not in the Take Care Clause. . . .

The President Is Not Above the Law

If the President does have a general power to violate treaties, then either treaties are not law or the President has the power to violate the law. The latter proposition is at odds with the principle that our government is "a government of laws, and not of men." As to the former proposition, it is true that some treaty provisions lack the status of law within our domestic legal system. . . . However, . . . most provisions of the Geneva Conventions are the law of the land. Therefore, a general presidential power to violate the Geneva Conventions would effectively mean that the President is above the law.

Advocates of a presidential power to violate treaties might seek to avert this consequence by distinguishing among different types of law. The federal constitution and statutes are binding on the President. In contrast, a President is free to disregard an executive order issued by his predecessor, even though such an executive order has the status of "law." One could argue that treaties are like executive orders,[5] because both derive from the President's Article II powers. Thus, the claim that Presidents have a general power to violate treaties does not imply that the President is above the law. Rather, the President's power to violate the law applies only to laws that are promulgated on the basis of the President's Article II powers.

This argument is unpersuasive. It is true that the Treaty Power is an Article II power, whereas Congress's legislative powers are derived from Article I. In this sense, treaties differ from statutes. Treaties are similar to statutes, however, in that they require the joint action of the executive and legislative branches. In contrast, an executive order can become law without any legislative participation. Thus, from a structural standpoint, the President should not be required to obtain congressional approval to violate an executive order because the President does not need such approval to adopt an executive order. On the other hand, the President must obtain legislative approval to violate a treaty provision that has the status of law because treaties require Senate approval in order to become law.

International Law Is in the U.S. Interest

Policy considerations support this constitutional analysis. The United States has a long-term interest in promoting the development of an international system that is governed increasingly by agreed-upon legal rules, and less by sheer power politics. On the other hand, the United States, more than any other nation in the world today, has the power to thwart the development of an effective international legal order by shun-

5. An executive order is an order issued by the president to direct executive officers.

ning the agreed-upon rules when it is convenient to do so. Moreover, there are many situations where short-term interests provide incentives for the United States to violate international law. From a constitutional standpoint, the best way to promote our long-term interest in fostering the development of the rule of law in the international sphere is to have constitutional arrangements that make it more difficult for the United States to renege on its international commitments. A constitutional rule that grants the President a general power to violate treaties would make it too easy for the United States to breach its treaty obligations. In contrast, a constitutional rule that requires the President to obtain legislative approval to violate a treaty makes it harder for the United States to violate treaties, and helps promote our long-term national interest in strengthening the rule of law internationally.

> *"There's substantial evidence that the United States routinely and knowingly 'outsources' the application of torture by transferring terrorism suspects to countries that frequently violate international human rights norms."*

Extraordinary Rendition Violates International Law

Sangitha McKenzie Millar

Sangitha McKenzie Millar is a research associate at Citizens for Global Solutions. In the following viewpoint, she argues that the United States uses extraordinary rendition to knowingly transfer suspects to countries where they will be tortured. Millar argues that this practice violates international law and U.S. law. Further, she maintains that it damages the United States' relationship with its allies and forfeits U.S. moral leadership. She argues that the practice should be stopped and restitution made to its victims.

Sangitha McKenzie Millar, "Extraordinary Rendition, Extraordinary Mistake," *Foreign Policy in Focus*, August 29, 2008. Copyright © 2008 Institute for Policy Studies. Reproduced by permission.

As you read, consider the following questions:

1. According to Aziz Huq, how was the post-9/11 extraordinary rendition system qualitatively different from earlier rendition programs?

2. According to Sangitha McKenzie Millar, as of the writing of her viewpoint, what was the status of Abdul Rahman Rashul?

3. Extraordinary rendition violates what specific U.S. law, according to Millar?

Mamdouh Habib, an Australian citizen, was living in Sydney with his wife and four children when he took a trip alone to Pakistan to find a home for his family. When Habib boarded a bus for the Islamabad airport to return home, Pakistani police seized him and took him to a police station, where he was subjected to various crude torture techniques, including electric shocks and beating. At one point, he was forced to hang by the arms above a drum-like mechanism that administered an electric shock when touched. Pakistani police asked him repeatedly if he was with al-Qaeda, and if he trained in Afghanistan. Habib responded "No" over and over until he passed out.

After 15 days in the Pakistani prison, Habib was transferred to U.S. agents who flew him to Cairo. When he arrived, Omar Solaimon, chief of Egyptian security, informed him that Egypt receives $10 million for every confessed terrorist they hand over to the United States. Habib stated that during his five months in Egypt, "there was no interrogation, only torture." His skin was burned with cigarettes and he was threatened with dogs, beaten, and repeatedly shocked with a stun gun. During this time, he heard American voices in the prison, but Egyptians were in charge of the torture. In Michael Otterman's book *American Torture: From the Cold War to Abu Ghraib and Beyond* [2007] . . . , Habib said he was drugged and began to hallucinate: "I feel like a dead person. I was gone. I become crazy." He remembers admitting things to interrogators, anything they asked: "I didn't care . . . at this point I was ready to die."

He was transferred back to the custody of U.S. agents in May 2002. They flew him first to Bagram Air Base in Afghanistan and then to Kandahar. After several weeks, American agents sent Habib to Guantánamo Bay. Three British detainees who have since been released from the prison described Habib as being in a "catastrophic state" when he arrived. Most of his fingernails were missing and he regularly bled from the nose, mouth, and ears while he slept.

Habib was held at Guantánamo Bay until late 2004, when he was charged with training 9/11 hijackers in martial arts, attending an al-Qaeda training camp in Afghanistan, and transporting chemical weapons. A Chicago human rights lawyer took his case and detailed all of Habib's allegations of torture in court documents. After the case garnered national attention through a front page story in *The Washington Post*, Habib became a liability for the U.S. government. Rather than have his testimony on the torture he suffered in Egypt become a matter of public record, U.S. officials decided to send him back to Sydney in January 2005—over three years after seizing him in Pakistan.

Outsourcing Torture

Unfortunately, Habib's case isn't unusual. There's substantial evidence that the United States routinely and knowingly "outsources" the application of torture by transferring terrorism suspects to countries that frequently violate international human rights norms. As details of the extraordinary rendition program have emerged, politicians, journalists, academics, legal experts, and policymakers have raised serious objections to the policy. . . .

The Origins of Extraordinary Rendition

At the most basic level, the term "rendition" refers to the practice of seizing and transferring a person from one country to another, usually for the purpose of criminal prosecution. Ordinary rendition is common in international relations and involves the surrendering of persons to foreign jurisdictions, in accordance with a treaty or enabling statute, and through a stipulated procedure. "Extraordinary rendition" involves [rendering] persons to non-judicial authorities outside of treaty and legal processes. This is usually accomplished through kidnapping and forced transfer from one country to another. "In many cases of extraordinary rendition, it appears that the seized persons are expressly delivered to foreign jurisdictions to circumvent . . . constitutional rights," write David Weissbrodt and Amy Bergquist. "They are rendered in a manner to specifically deprive them of due process and civil liberties protections." In contrast to extradition, the suspect does not go through the legal system of the country where he is arrested. These persons are sometimes called "ghost detainees" and are outside the protections of domestic or international law in any practical sense.

Extraordinary rendition evolved out of pre-9/11 practices intended to facilitate judicial processes. Only after 9/11 [the terrorist attacks of September 11, 2001] did it become a purposive way to evade U.S. legal prohibitions against torture. In fact, the United States has practiced ordinary rendition since the 1800s, rendering criminal suspects from overseas to be tried in the United States, and these prosecutions were twice endorsed by the U.S. Supreme Court. However, in the 1980s, the United States began rendering suspects to other countries as well, in order to expand counterterrorism efforts. In the 1990s, CIA [Central Intelligence Agency] officers reportedly collaborated with Egyptian interrogators to such an extent that U.S. officials would provide their Egyptian counterparts with a list of questions in the morning and would receive answers by evening—illustrating how the United States encouraged and relied on Egyptian interrogation techniques. Former CIA official Michael Scheuer ran rendition operations from 1995 until 1999 and takes credit for creating the extraordinary rendition program in 1995.

The first suspect sent to Egypt was Talaat Fouad Qassem, an Egyptian linked to the [1981] assassination of Egyptian President Anwar Sadat. In late 1995 he was kidnapped in Croatia, interrogated by U.S. agents on a ship on the Adriatic Sea, and then handed over to Egypt. Human rights experts believe he was tortured, then executed—no record of any trial exists. "When the CIA delivered Talaat Fouad Qassem to the Egyptian authorities, it was certainly aware of how he would be treated," writes Aziz Z. Huq. . . .

According to a former FBI [Federal Bureau of Investigation] interrogator in Otterman's book, after the 9/11 attacks, rendition "really went out of control." In the aftermath of the attacks the program has accelerated, in part due to expedited procedures approved by President George W. Bush, affording more flexibility to the CIA. On September 17, 2001, America's rendition policy changed in scale and purpose when Bush signed a secret presidential finding that authorized the CIA to capture, kill, or detain members of al-Qaeda anywhere in the world. "The administration's avowed aim was to allow the transfer of suspects to jurisdictions with laxer constraints on coercive interrogation," writes Huq. "Torture thus became a primary goal, not merely a collateral consequence, of rendition to third countries. In this respect, the post-9/11 extraordinary rendition system is qualitatively different from the rendition programs that preceded it."

By late 2001, the CIA was inundated with prisoners captured in Afghanistan during Operation Enduring Freedom. The U.S.-led campaign had netted thousands of detainees. According to several reports, the CIA and other intelligence agencies have up to 100 high-value detainees in custody held "off the books" in unknown locations. Of the approximately 100 detainees believed to have been "rendered" in the last six years, 39 remain unaccounted for. According to former attorney general Alberto Gonzales, "We do not transport anyone to a country if we believe it more likely than not that the individual will be tortured." However, as Otterman notes, an official quoted in *The Washington Post* explained it differently: "We don't kick the [expletive] out of them. We send them to other countries so they can kick the [expletive] out of them." Scheuer, father of the extraordinary rendition program, concedes that "the bar was lowered after 9/11."

Egypt, Syria, and Black Sites

The opaque and confidential nature of the CIA's covert program of extraordinary renditions is perhaps best illustrated by the case involving Iraqi national Hiwa Abdul Rahman Rashul. In summer 2003, Kurdish soldiers captured Rashul in Iraq and handed him over to CIA agents, who flew him to Afghanistan for interrogation. Rashul was flown back to Iraq after a legal advisor for the U.S. administration balked at the transfer. At this point then-Secretary of Defense Donald Rumsfeld, at the behest of then-CIA director George Tenet, ordered that Rashul be hidden from the International Committee of the Red Cross[1] and not be given a prisoner number. His status remains unknown.

Suspects sent abroad for interrogation have returned with horrific tales of abuse. One example is Canadian software engineer Maher Arar, who was held in Syria for almost a year in a basement cell less than one meter wide by two meters deep. Arar notes in Otterman's book he was regularly beaten by Syrian interrogators: "The cable [was] a black electrical cable, about two inches thick. They hit me with it everywhere on my body. They mostly aimed for my palms, but sometimes missed

---

1. The International Committee of the Red Cross is a humanitarian organization that investigates and reports on the condition of prisoners captured in conflicts.

and hit my wrists; they were sore and red for three weeks. They also struck me on my hips and lower back. . . . I could hear other prisoners being tortured, and screaming and screaming." After Arar's release in October 2003, the Syrian ambassador to the United States conceded that Syria had found no evidence of Arar's complicity in terrorism. Top-level officials have admitted that the program is attractive for dealing with terrorists. Tenet testified before Congress, "It might be better sometimes for . . . suspects to remain in the hands of foreign authorities, who might be able to use more aggressive interrogation techniques" and Vice President Dick Cheney has said that when dealing with terrorism, "We're operating through sort of, you know, a dark side."

The extraordinary rendition program sends suspects to countries with atrocious human rights records, such as Egypt and Syria, both of which have been consistently cited in U.S. State Department reports for using torture. As early as 1994, the State Department concluded that in Egypt, "torture is used to extract information. . . . Detainees are frequently stripped to their underwear; hung by their wrists with their feet touching the floor or forced to stand for prolonged periods; doused with hot and cold water; beaten; forced to stand outdoors in cold weather; and subjected to electric shocks.". . .

However, not all suspects are rendered to foreign security forces. Some are sent to "black sites," secret prisons run by the CIA in various nations. As the number of detainees increased after 2001, renditions could not keep up. The CIA requested and received hundreds of millions of dollars to start construction of a private CIA prison network. The Military Commissions Act of 2006 legalized the interrogation techniques employed by CIA agents at these black sites, which include hypothermia, forced standing, sleep deprivation, and simulated drowning, according to Otterman. At a black site in Afghanistan known as the "Salt Pit," an Afghan detainee was stripped naked, chained to a concrete floor outside his cell, and left there overnight. He died of hypothermia and was buried in an unmarked grave near the prison. Otterman notes that no one has been charged with his death, and the agent directing the interrogation has since been promoted.

Rhetoric vs. Reality

Increasing criticism of extraordinary rendition has caused governmental officials to go on the defensive, assuring the public that the program does not aim to transfer suspects to have them tortured. In March 2005, Bush stated that the goal of extraordinary rendition was "to arrest people and send them back to their country of origin with the promise that they won't be tortured. That's the promise we receive." He also stated that the United States was leading the fight against torture by example, and that "torture is never acceptable, nor do we hand over people to countries that do torture.". . .

However, the contrast between the official rhetoric and the reality of the extraordinary rendition program is glaring. In practice, argues Daniel Byman of Georgetown University, "U.S. officials may seek to transfer suspects from a Western ally to the Middle East because the Western ally's laws or inclinations prevent the close monitoring or aggressive interrogation of a terrorism suspect—in contrast to many Middle Eastern countries with poor human rights records. . . . Many U.S. allies in the Middle East have a far lower standard of evidence and are willing to bend what rules they have in response to a U.S. request . . . [s]ome Middle Eastern countries can also persuade or coerce a suspect's relatives." Despite the governmental rhetoric on the issue, documented cases of extraordinary rendition present a much darker picture of the practice.

Government officials speak of written "diplomatic assurances" that suspects will not be tortured. However, Michael Scheuer, former chief of the CIA's counterterrorism unit that established the extraordinary rendition program, has said that he was "not sure" whether any such assurances were signed before suspects were transferred. Scheuer also stated that he regularly told senior lawyers and policymakers that "Egypt was Egypt" and that in response they inserted a "legal nicety" into the extraordinary rendition procedures. Another CIA agent called these promises a "farce," and an unnamed official told *The Washington Post*, "They say they are not abusing them, and that satisfies the legal requirement, but we all know they do." . . .

There is also no evidence to suggest that the United States has ever protested to Syria, Egypt, or any other of its extraordinary rendition partners about torture after transfer. . . .

Illegal and Unpopular

Extraordinary rendition violates both international and U.S. domestic law. In terms of international law, a 2006 study analyzing extraordinary rendition from a human rights perspective concluded that the practice "violates numerous international human rights standards, including the Universal Declaration of Human Rights, the International Covenant on Civil and Political Rights, the International Covenant on Economic, Social and Cultural Rights, the Convention and Protocol Relating to the Status of Refugees, the Convention Against Torture, the Vienna Convention on Consular Relations, and the Geneva Conventions."[2]

The Universal Declaration of Human Rights guarantees the "right to life, liberty, and security of the person," and some argue that extraordinary rendition violates the treaty because the abduction itself involves a deprivation of liberty and security. Furthermore, the Declaration guarantees that "Everyone has the right to recognition everywhere as a person before the law," but extraordinary rendition denies individuals access to judicial procedures and legal recognition. Extraordinary rendi-

2. The Geneva Conventions are international laws regulating the conduct of states in wartime.

tion also violates the Geneva Conventions of 1949 in that Article 49 prohibits forcible transportations and deportations "regardless of their motive."

Additionally, the Convention Against Torture and Other Cruel, Inhuman or Degrading Treatment or Punishment (CAT) prohibits sending an individual to a state where there are substantial grounds to believe that the person would be in danger of being tortured. The United States has both signed and ratified the treaty, which directs signatories to "take into account all relevant considerations including, where applicable, the existence in the State concerned of a consistent pattern of gross, flagrant, or mass violations of human rights.". . .

Although much of the current discourse surrounding extraordinary rendition concerns international law, the practice violates U.S. law as well. The 1998 Foreign Affairs Reform and Restructuring Act (FARRA) states: "It shall be the policy of the United States not to expel, extradite, or otherwise affect the involuntary return of any person to a country in which there are substantial grounds for believing the person would be in danger of being subjected to torture." . . .

Undermining the National Interest

Disputes over extraordinary rendition have resulted in tangible setbacks for the United States in terms of weakening relationships with allies, undermining the growth of democracy in the Middle East, undercutting counterterrorism efforts, and giving al-Qaeda a powerful recruiting tool.

Among U.S. allies, as information on the extraordinary rendition program came to light, politicians and journalists roundly condemned the practice. [U.S. Secretary of State Condoleezza] Rice's visit to Europe in 2005 and defense of extraordinary rendition only served to widen the trans-Atlantic divide on the issue. So far, Germany has issued arrest warrants for 13 U.S. intelligence officers. Italy has indicted 26 Ameri-

No Law for Detainees

For ten years, [Federal Bureau of Investigation (FBI) agent Dan] Coleman worked closely with the CIA [Central Intelligence Agency] on counter-terrorism cases, including the [1998] Embassy attacks in Kenya and Tanzania. His methodical style of detective work, in which interrogations were aimed at forging relationships with detainees, became unfashionable after [the terrorist attacks of] September 11th, [2001], in part because the government was intent on extracting information as quickly as possible, in order to prevent future attacks. Yet the more patient approach used by Coleman and other agents had yielded major successes. In the Embassy-bombings case, they helped convict four Al Qaeda operatives on three hundred and two criminal counts; all four men pleaded guilty to serious terrorism charges. The confessions the FBI agents elicited, and the trial itself, which ended in May 2001, created an invaluable public record about Al Qaeda including details about its funding mechanisms, its internal structure, and its intention to obtain weapons of mass destruction. . . .

Coleman is a political nonpartisan with a law-and-order mentality. . . . Yet Coleman was troubled by the [George W.] Bush Administration's New Paradigm. Torture, he said, "has become bureaucratized." Bad as the policy of rendition was before September 11th, Coleman said, "afterward, it really went out of control." He explained, "Now, instead of just sending people to third countries, we're holding them ourselves. We're taking people, and keeping them in our own custody in third countries. That's an enormous problem." Egypt, he pointed out, at least had an established legal system, however harsh.

Jane Mayer, "Outsourcing Torture," The New Yorker, *February 14, 2005. www.newyorker.com.*

cans for their alleged role in the 2003 extradition of Egyptian cleric Hassan Mustafa Osama Nasr.

Nasr was abducted from Milan and then transferred to Egypt where he asserts he was badly tortured. According to Human Rights Watch, the prosecution represents the first ever legal challenge to the extraordinary rendition program, and the American defendants will be tried in absentia. Additionally, a Canadian government commission has censured the United States for Maher Arar's rendition, and the Council of Europe and the European Union have each issued reports critical of the U.S. rendition program. In July 2007, the United Kingdom issued a report concluding that the practice would have "serious implications" for future intelligence relations between the United States and United Kingdom. . . .

As criticism of extraordinary rendition continues to mount some important American allies, such as Great Britain, Canada, and Germany, seized the opportunity to denounce the practice and have ordered investigations into allegations of previous complicity in the program. However, some Eastern European nations, such as Poland and Romania, are suspected of continued collaboration with CIA agents involved in extraordinary rendition despite the growing international opposition to the practice.

As important [as] the impact of extraordinary rendition is on our European allies, it is perhaps more influential on our undemocratic partners in the Middle East. Circumventing legal channels weakens international judicial and prosecutorial cooperation, which makes the rule of law in countries such as Egypt and Syria even more vulnerable. For example, since 1952 Egypt has suffered under total executive domination, wherein dissension is subdued by extralegal methods and sometimes through violent repression by security forces. "Egyptian-American cooperation in extraordinary rendition strengthens the least law-abiding elements of the Egyptian state, its internal security forces, and thus corrodes the prospects for full Egyptian democracy," writes Huq.

Additionally, the United States encourages human rights violators to continue to torture through the extraordinary rendition program. This has proved true in Sudan and Zimbabwe, which have justified "disappearances" of foes to the ruling regimes on the grounds that the U.S. also "disappears" people. Zimbabwe's representative to the U.N. Human Rights Commission brushed off American criticism of abuses by his government, saying, "Those who live in a glass house should not throw stones. . . . [America has] a lot of dirt on its hands." Additionally, in a meeting with representatives from Human Rights Watch, Egyptian Prime Minister Ahmed Nazif responded to allegation[s] of torture on the part of his security forces by stating, "We're just doing what the United States does."

Not only does extraordinary rendition empower local factions who are opposed to the development of democracy, it is also a powerful recruiting tool for al-Qaeda. In a hearing before the Senate Committee on Foreign Relations, Chairman Joseph Biden asserted, "In our long-term effort to stem the tide of international terrorism, our commitments to the rule of law and to individual rights and civil liberties are among our most formidable weapons . . . the controversial aspects of the United States government's use of rendition have been used by propagandists and recruiters to fuel and sustain international terrorist organizations with a constant stream of new recruits."

Extraordinary rendition has also made cooperation between U.S. and European police and intelligence agencies more difficult. Faced with public pressure over reports that European intelligence services were collaborating with U.S. agents in extraordinary renditions, European police and judiciaries have limited the scope of counterterrorism cooperation. Extraordinary rendition also undermines the recommendations of the 9/11 Commission,[3] which emphasized the need for the United States to "offer an example of moral leadership in the world, committed to treat people humanely, abide by the rule of law, and be generous and caring to our neighbors.". . .

End Extraordinary Rendition

Ultimately, the U.S. policy of extraordinary rendition relies on disingenuous diplomatic assurances and can result in the torture and prolonged detention of innocent individuals. It also tarnishes our reputation in the international community and undermines American national interests by alienating our allies and weakening counterterrorism efforts. Accordingly, the next administration needs to definitively and publicly end the extraordinary rendition program. In addition, there needs to be some level of accountability in terms of recognizing how and where erroneous renditions have occurred and providing appropriate compensation. One place to start would be with Maher Arar, who should immediately be removed from the U.S. terrorist watch-lists and appropriately compensated for his suffering.

3. The National Commission on Terrorist Attacks upon the United States, also known as the 9/11 Commission, was an independent, nonpartisan commission created by Congressional legislation and President George W. Bush in 2002 in order to prepare a full and complete account of the circumstances surrounding the September 11, 2001, terrorist attacks.

| "*Washington . . . must maintain the suc-cessful policy of rendition, a vital weapon in the defense of the West.*"

Rendition Does Not Violate International Law

Niles Gardiner and James Jay Carafano

Niles Gardiner is a fellow at the Margaret Thatcher Center for Freedom; James Jay Carafano is a research fellow at the Heritage Foundation. In the following viewpoint, they argue that rendition of suspects to third-world countries is a vital policy in containing and obtaining information from terrorists. They maintain that rendition does not result in torture and that it is legal. They contend that European opposition to rendition is based on anti-U.S. bias. America, they say, should therefore ignore the outcry from pan-European organizations, such as the European Union, and should instead concentrate on working with more cooperative individual European states.

As you read, consider the following questions:

1. What sparked the spat between the United States and the European Union over renditions, according to Niles Gardiner and James Jay Carafano?

Niles Gardiner and James Jay Carafano, "The Great EU Inquisition: Europe's Response to the U.S. Rendition Policy," Heritage Foundation Web Memo, February 6, 2006. Reproduced by permission.

2. According to Gardiner and Carafano, did the Council of Europe report on rendition in January 2006 find any evidence of secret Central Intelligence Agency detention centers in any Eastern European country?

3. According to the authors why do rendition programs operate in secrecy?

"We do not have a war against terror." This extraordinary statement by a senior European Union (EU) official reflects the divide between Washington and Europe's leading political institutions over the fight against al-Qaeda. Despite three major terrorist attacks on European soil in the past three years [2003 to 2006] (in London, Madrid, and Istanbul), many top European officials still do not grasp the magnitude of the terrorist threat. Instead, they are engaged in a campaign of pandering and grandstanding to delegitimize U.S. counter-terrorism efforts, especially the policy of rendition.

The Council of Europe, which oversees the European Court of Human Rights, has already released a flimsy report on rendition,[1] and the European Parliament has launched its own investigation. These supranational institutions' anti-American animus reinforces the need for the U.S. to oppose "ever-closer union" in Europe. While U.S.-EU relations have been damaged by the rendition controversy, Washington should continue to work closely with the governments of individual European states and must maintain the successful policy of rendition, a vital weapon in the defense of the West. Officials from the United States and European nation-states should unite in castigating the EU-Council of Europe witch-hunt, which is widening the transatlantic divide.

1. Rendition is the practice of transferring detainees to other countries to be held or interrogated.

Anti-U.S. Bias

The leaders of al-Qaeda and the many other Islamic terrorist organizations that operate across the globe will no doubt warmly welcome the latest attempts by European officials to rein in the U.S.-led war on terrorism.

The European Parliament in Strasbourg has launched a 46-member inquiry into "the alleged illegal transfer of detainees and the suspected existence of secret CIA [Central Intelligence Agency] detention facilities in the European Union and in candidate countries," with members haggling for "much-coveted seats" on the investigative committee. Baroness Sarah Ludford, vice chairman of the committee . . . has pledged to leave "no stone unturned" in "upholding the core values of human rights which lie at the heart of the union" and has urged senior U.S. officials to face hearings in Europe. In a major affront to U.S. sovereignty and a demonstration of breathtaking arrogance, Vice President Dick Cheney and Secretary of Defense Donald Rumsfeld have been called upon to testify before the committee.

There is little doubt that the inquiry will feed upon widespread anti-American sentiment in the European Parliament and will be used to batter U.S. counter-terrorism strategy. As one British Conservative Member of the European Parliament put it, the inquiry will likely serve as "a platform for anti-U.S. bile."

The U.S.-EU spat was sparked by an article in *The Washington Post* which alleged that the Central Intelligence Agency (CIA) ran a covert prison, or "black site," for senior al-Qaeda suspects at a Soviet-era compound in Eastern Europe as part of a "hidden global internment network." The *Post* article also charged that scores of detainees had been "delivered to intelligence services in Egypt, Jordan, Morocco, Afghanistan and other countries, [in] a process sometimes known as 'rendition.'" The U.S.-based Human Rights Watch later claimed that the CIA was operating secret detention facilities in Poland and Romania.

These reports prompted moral indignation and mass hysteria among the political elites of Brussels and Strasbourg[2] and led to sensational accusations that the United States tortured terror suspects while holding them in 'gulags,' with the connivance of Eastern European governments. Some alleged that the U.S. flew terror suspects to countries in North Africa and the Middle East for the specific purpose of torture.

This controversy led to an undignified political power play by federal European politicians who seek to dictate the security policy of European nation-states. With echoes of French President Jacques Chirac's infamous threat to aspiring EU members in Eastern Europe who had supported the United States over the war with Iraq, the European Union's Justice Minister Franco Frattini warned of "serious consequences, including the suspension of voting rights in the council," for any EU member-state found to have hosted secret CIA facilities.

In addition, the United Nations [UN], with its hugely discredited human rights apparatus in tow, could not resist the opportunity to take a swipe at the United States. Louise Arbour, the UN's High Commissioner for Human Rights, launched a fierce attack on America's "so-called war on terrorism," condemning U.S. interrogation techniques and the rendition of terrorist suspects. While millions languish under the boot of brutal dictatorships from Rangoon to Pyongyang to Tehran, the UN's chief concern on its "Human Rights Day" last December was U.S. tactics in the battle against the most barbaric terrorist movement in modern history.

The European Parliament's investigation follows a major inquiry by the Council of Europe, which published its initial findings in late January [2006]. In presenting his report, Dick Marty, the Council's Rapporteur, condemned the "gangster-style methods" of the [George W.] Bush Administration, stating that "individuals have been abducted, deprived of their liberty and all rights, and transported to different destinations

2. Brussels and Strasbourg are political centers of the European Union.

in Europe, to be handed over to countries in which they have suffered degrading treatment and torture."

On closer examination however, Marty's case is paper-thin and lacks any concrete evidence. If this case were presented in a court of law, it would be dismissed out of hand. In the words of Denis MacShane, the UK's [United Kingdom's] former Minister for Europe, the report has "more holes than a Swiss cheese."

Marty's report contains no primary source documentation and relies entirely upon media accounts. It is filled with con-jecture, innuendo, and a barely disguised sneering contempt for the U.S. approach to the war on terrorism. For example, Marty concludes that "the current U.S. Administration seems to start from the principle that the principles of the rule of law and human rights are incompatible with efficient action against terrorism," a clear misrepresentation of the U.S. position.

Significantly, the Council of Europe's report admits, "At this stage of the investigations, there is no formal, irrefutable evidence of the existence of secret CIA detention centers in Romania, Poland or any other country." It cites the findings of an investigation appointed by the Romanian Parliament and conducted by OADO, a human rights NGO [non-governmental organization], that "do not seem to provide any evidence of such centers." Nevertheless, the report freely cites rumors and circumstantial and highly ambiguous facts as justification for condemning U.S. efforts to protect itself and its allies against terrorist attacks.

U.S. Rendition Policy

The U.S. practice of rendition dates back to the mid-1990s and was established by the [Bill] Clinton Administration to target al-Qaeda cells operating across the world. Rendition involves the capture of terrorist suspects, who are brought to

America Is Not the Threat

Respondees in the latest attitudes poll undertaken in the five major Member States of the European Union—Britain, France, Germany, Italy and Spain—see the United States as the world's biggest security risk.

These results are alarming, and show a profound level of moral and conceptual exhaustion on the part of many Europeans. Imagining that America is a bigger danger than Russia, Iran or China is a self-indulgence of the worst kind.

James Rogers, "The Poverty of Anti-Americanism,"
Global Power Europe, *July 2, 2007. www.globalpowereurope.eu.*

the United States to face trial or are transferred to the governments of their home countries for further questioning.

The policy has three main goals:

- Keep terror suspects off the streets,

- Bring to justice those wanted for terrorist offences, and

- Gather valuable intelligence information about possible future terror attacks.

The CIA and FBI [Federal Bureau of Investigation] put rendition to good use in June 1997 in the capture in Pakistan of Mr Aimal Kasi, who was brought back to America to face trial for the 1993 murder of two CIA employees in Virginia. According to then-CIA Director George Tenet, more than two-dozen terrorists, half of them al-Qaeda suspects, were brought to justice by rendition between July 1998 and February 2000. A number of European governments also employ rendition. France, for example, captured Carlos the Jackal in Sudan in 1994 and brought him to France to face trial; this operation was deemed lawful by the European Court of Human Rights. After [the terrorist attacks of September 11, 2001] the United States greatly expanded its use of rendition. Between 100 and 150 major terrorist suspects have been apprehended under the policy since 9/11.

The U.S. rendition policy is not intended to facilitate the torture of detained suspects. Torture is against U.S. law, and government policy requires that American officials must obtain assurances from countries where detainees might be transferred that no methods contrary to international and U.S. law will be employed.

That these programs are secret does not imply that they are illegal or conducted without the cooperation of the sovereign nations through which detained individuals may transit or in which they may be temporarily detained. Secrecy protects the personnel who transport these potentially dangerous prisoners. It also prevents terrorists from gaining any operational advantage by knowing who has been recently detained.

Finally, there is no credible evidence that renditions have been used in conjunction with 'secret prisons' in Eastern Europe. There is no clear operational need for such prisons. The United States openly maintains a long-term detention facility at Guantanamo Bay that is run in accordance with U.S. law and abides by relevant international treaties.

Significantly, British Prime Minister Tony Blair has strongly supported U.S. statements that the policy of rendition has not been used to facilitate the torture of terror suspects in other countries and has firmly rejected calls for a British parliamentary inquiry. In a response to the House of Commons, Blair stated:

> Let me draw a very clear distinction indeed between the idea of suspects being taken from one country to another and any sense whatever that ourselves, the United States or anyone condones the use of torture. Torture cannot be justified in any set of circumstances at all. The practice of rendi-

tion as described by [U.S.] Secretary of State Condoleezza Rice has been American policy for many years. We have not had such a situation here, but that has been American policy for many, many years. However, it must be applied in accordance with international conventions, and I accept entirely Secretary of State Rice's assurance that it has been.

Ignore European Objections

The rendition controversy has seriously damaged the United States' working relationship with the EU in the war on terrorism. However, it should not weaken the ability of the United States to cooperate effectively with individual European nation-states, which have strongly supported U.S. efforts in the war on terrorism. Nor should it discourage the United States from continuing to use rendition, which has proved a very effective mechanism.

A key lesson that the United States should take away from the rendition debate is that the increasing political centralization of Europe poses a fundamental threat to U.S. interests. Washington must support a Europe of nation-states and stop paying lip-service to the Franco-German dream of ever-closer integration. The United States works most effectively when it cooperates directly with national governments in Europe, employing a 'coalition of the willing' strategy. Europe is not and never has been a united political entity, and U.S. policy must support national sovereignty in Europe. Washington's political capital in Europe must be spent not in Brussels or Strasbourg, but in the national capitals, where America's strongest allies are to be found.

Rendition has proved a highly effective tool in the war against terrorism and has pulled hundreds of extremely dangerous terror suspects off the streets. In all probability, many lives, both American and European, have been saved by this practice. The West is engaged in an epic war against Islamic extremists who will give no quarter, whether in London, Brussels, New York, or Baghdad. The policy of rendition is a response to this reality.

European Union officials and Members of the European Parliament should stop using the war on terrorism as an elaborate public relations exercise and cease wielding it as a stick with which to beat U.S. foreign policy.

The United States must continue to pursue aggressively those who threaten the security of the free world and should continue to work closely with individual European governments in the fight against al-Qaeda and other Islamic terrorist groups. Most importantly, the U.S. must resist the temptation to blunt its most effective weapons in the face of criticism from the EU, the UN, and other supranational institutions.

> *"The suggestion that the Bush admini-*
> *stration's conduct in the 'war on terror'*
> *amounts to a string of war crimes and*
> *human rights abuses is gaining cre-*
> *dence in even the most ossified estab-*
> *lishment circles of Washington."*

The President Should Be Held Accountable by International Courts

Jan Frel

Jan Frel is a former senior editor at AlterNet *and a contributor to* Personal Democracy Forum. *In the following viewpoint, he argues that the U.S. invasion of Iraq was an act of aggressive war not authorized by the United Nations Security Council, and that, as such, it constitutes a war crime. Frel also suggests that George W. Bush administration violations of the Geneva Conventions in dealing with detainees could qualify as war crimes. Frel admits that there is little possibility that American officials will actually face international trial, though he hopes that it might be a possibility.*

Jan Frel, "Could Bush Be Prosecuted for War Crimes?" *AlterNet*, July 10, 2006. Reproduced by permission.

As you read, consider the following questions:

1. Who is Benjamin Ferencz?

2. Did the first President Bush, George Herbert Walker Bush, believe that security council resolutions authorized an invasion of Iraq, according to Ferencz?

3. Is the United States a signatory and under jurisdiction of the International Criminal Court (ICC)?

The extent to which American exceptionalism is embedded in the national psyche is awesome to behold.

While the United States is a country like any other, its citizens no more special than any others on the planet, Americans still react with surprise at the suggestion that their country could be held responsible for something as heinous as a war crime.

U.S. War Crimes

From the massacre of more than 100,000 people in the Philippines [1901] to the first nuclear attack ever at Hiroshima [1945] to the unprovoked invasion of Baghdad [2003], U.S.-sponsored violence doesn't feel as wrong and worthy of prosecution in internationally sanctioned criminal courts as the gory, bload-soaked atrocities of Congo, Darfur, Rwanda, and most certainly not the Nazis—most certainly not. [American historian] Howard Zinn recently described this as our "inability to think outside the boundaries of nationalism. We are penned in by the arrogant idea that this country is the center of the universe, exceptionally virtuous, admirable, superior."

Most Americans firmly believe there is nothing the United States or its political leadership could possibly do that could equate to the crimes of Hitler's Third Reich. The Nazis are our "gold standard of evil," as author John Dolan once put it.

But the truth is that we can, and we have—most recently and significantly in Iraq. Perhaps no person on the planet is better equipped to identify and describe our crimes in Iraq than Benjamin Ferencz, a former chief prosecutor of the Nuremberg Trials who successfully convicted 22 Nazi officers for their work in orchestrating death squads that killed more than one million people in the famous Einsatzgruppen Case. Ferencz, now 87, has gone on to become a founding father of the basis behind international law regarding war crimes, and his essays and legal work drawing from the Nuremberg trials and later the commission that established the International Criminal Court remain a lasting influence in that realm.

Ferencz's biggest contribution to the war crimes field is his assertion that an unprovoked or "aggressive" war is the highest crime against mankind. It was the decision to invade Iraq in 2003 that made possible the horrors of Abu Ghraib, the destruction of Fallouja and Ramadi,[1] the tens of thousands of Iraqi deaths, civilian massacres like Haditha[2] and on and on. Ferencz believes that a "prima facie case can be made that the United States is guilty of the supreme crime against humanity, that being an illegal war of aggression against a sovereign nation."

The Case Against the United States

Interviewed from his home in New York, Ferencz laid out a simple summary of the case:

> The United Nations [U.N.] charter has a provision which was agreed to by the United States, formulated by the United States in fact, after World War II. It says that from now on, no nation can use armed force without the permission of the U.N. Security Council. They can use force in connection with self-defense, but a country can't use force in *anticipa-*

---

1. Abu Ghraib was a prison in Iraq where American personnel tortured prisoners. Fallouja in Iraq was the site of a massive U.S. offensive in 2004 during which human rights abuses have been alleged. Ramadi was also the scene of heavy fighting.
2. In 2005, U.S. Marines killed 24 people in Haditha, Iraq, most of them noncombatant civilians.

tion of self-defense. Regarding Iraq, the last Security Council resolution essentially said, 'Look, send the weapons inspectors out to Iraq, have them come back and tell us what they've found—then we'll figure out what we're going to do. The U.S. was impatient, and decided to invade Iraq—which was all pre-arranged of course. So, the United States went to war, in violation of the charter.

It's that simple. Ferencz called the invasion a "clear breach of law," and dismissed the [George W.] Bush administration's legal defense that previous U.N. Security Council resolutions dating back to the first Gulf War justified an invasion in 2003. Ferencz notes that the first Bush president [George H.W. Bush] believed that the United States didn't have a U.N. mandate to go into Iraq and take out Saddam Hussein; that authorization was simply to eject Hussein from Kuwait. Ferencz asked, "So how do we get authorization more than a decade later to finish the job? The arguments made to defend this are not persuasive."

Writing for the United Kingdom's *Guardian*, shortly before the 2003 invasion, international law expert Mark Littman echoed Ferencz: "The threatened war against Iraq will be a breach of the United Nations Charter and hence of international law unless it is authorized by a new and unambiguous resolution of the Security Council. The Charter is clear. No such war is permitted unless it is in self-defense or authorized by the Security Council."

Challenges to the legality of this war can also be found at the ground level. First Lt. Ehren Watada, the first U.S. commissioned officer to refuse to serve in Iraq, cites the rules of the U.N. Charter as a principle reason for his dissent.

Ferencz isn't using the invasion of Iraq as a convenient prop to exercise his longstanding American hatred: he has a decades-old paper trail of calls for every suspect of war crimes to be brought to international justice. When the United States captured Saddam Hussein in December 2003, Ferencz wrote that Hussein's offenses included "the supreme international crime of aggression, to a wide variety of crimes against humanity, and a long list of atrocities condemned by both international and national laws."

Ferencz isn't the first to make the suggestion that the United States has committed state-sponsored war crimes against another nation—not only have leading war critics made this argument, but so had legal experts in the British government before the 2003 invasion. In a short essay in 2005, Ferencz lays out the inner deliberations of British and American officials as the preparations for the war were made:

> U.K. military leaders had been calling for clear assurances that the war was legal under international law. They were very mindful that the treaty creating a new International Criminal Court (ICC) in The Hague had entered into force on July 1, 2002, with full support of the British government. Gen. Sir Mike Jackson, chief of the defense staff, was quoted as saying "I spent a good deal of time recently in the Balkans making sure Milosevic was put behind bars. I have no intention of ending up in the next cell to him in The Hague."

Ferencz quotes the British deputy legal adviser to the Foreign Ministry who, in the lead-up to the invasion, quit abruptly and wrote in her resignation letter: "I regret that I cannot agree that it is lawful to use force against Iraq without a second Security Council resolution. . . . [A]n unlawful use of force on such a scale amounts to the crime of aggression; nor can I agree with such action in circumstances that are so detrimental to the international order and the rule of law."

Prosecutions Are Unlikely

While the United Kingdom is a signatory of the ICC, and therefore under jurisdiction of that court, the United States is not, thanks to a Republican majority in Congress that has "attacks on America's sovereignty" and "manipulation by the United Nations" in its pantheon of knee-jerk neuroses. Fer-

The Haditha Massacre

On the morning of Nov. 19, 2005, a roadside bomb struck a humvee carrying Marines from Kilo Company, 3rd Battalion, 1st Marines, on a road near Haditha, a restive town in western Iraq. The bomb killed Lance Corporal Miguel (T.J.) Terrazas, 20, from El Paso, Texas. The next day a Marine communique from Camp Blue Diamond in Ramadi reported that Terrazas and 15 Iraqi civilians were killed by the blast and that "gunmen attacked the convoy with small-arms fire," prompting the Marines to return fire, killing eight insurgents and wounding one other. . . .

But the details of what happened that morning in Haditha are more disturbing, disputed and horrific than the military initially reported. According to eyewitnesses and local officials interviewed over the past 10 weeks [in early 2006], the civilians who died in Haditha on Nov. 19 were killed not by a roadside bomb but by the Marines themselves, who went on a rampage in the village after the attack, killing 15 unarmed Iraqis in their homes, including seven women and three children. Human-rights activists say that if the accusations are true, the incident ranks as the worst case of deliberate killing of Iraqi civilians by U.S. service members since the war began.

Tim McGirk,
"Collateral Damage or Civilian Massacre in Haditha?"
Time, *March 19, 2006. www.time.com.*

encz concedes that even though Britain and its leadership could be prosecuted, the international legal climate isn't at a place where justice is blind enough to try it—or as Ferencz put it, humanity isn't yet "civilized enough to prevent this type of illegal behavior." And Ferencz said that while he believes the United States is guilty of war crimes, "the international community is not sufficiently organized to prosecute such a case. . . . There is no court at the moment that is competent to try that crime."

As Ferencz said, the world is still a long way away from establishing norms that put all nations under the rule of law, but the battle to do so is a worthy one: "There's no such thing as a war without atrocities, but war-making is the biggest atrocity of all."

The suggestion that the Bush administration's conduct in the "war on terror" amounts to a string of war crimes and human rights abuses is gaining credence in even the most ossified establishment circles of Washington. Justice Anthony Kennedy's opinion in the recent *Hamdan v. Rumsfeld*[3] ruling by the Supreme Court suggests that Bush's attempt to ignore the Geneva Conventions[4] in his approved treatment of terror suspects may leave him open to prosecution for war crimes. As Sidney Blumenthal points out, the Court rejected Bush's attempt to ignore Common Article 3, which bans "cruel treatment and torture [and] outrages upon personal dignity, in particular humiliating and degrading treatment."

And since Congress enacted the Geneva Conventions, making them the law of the United States, any violations that Bush or any other American commits "are considered 'war crimes' punishable as federal offenses," as Justice Kennedy wrote.

George W. Bush in the dock facing a charge of war crimes? That's well beyond the scope of possibility . . . or is it?

3. *Hamdan v. Rumsfeld* was a 2006 Supreme Court case in which the court ruled that military commissions established by the Bush administration to try detainees violated the Geneva Conventions.
4. The Geneva Conventions are international laws regulating the conduct of states in war time.

| "There have always been serious concerns that the ICC [International Criminal Court] could investigate and try to indict American political, military, and intelligence officials for actions taken in defense of our country."

The President Should Not Be Answerable to International Law

Andrew C. McCarthy

Andrew C. McCarthy is a former assistant U.S. attorney known for his prosecution of terrorism suspects, and he is currently a senior fellow at the Foundation for Defense of Democracies. In the following viewpoint, he argues that President Barack Obama's administration would like international bodies to indict officials from the George W. Bush administration. McCarthy believes Obama wants to prosecute Bush, but fears that the domestic fallout would be too great. In addition, McCarthy maintains, Obama wants to strengthen the international regime. McCarthy argues that this plan will damage American sovereignty and punish those who tried to defend the country.

Andrew C. McCarthy, "Eric Holder's Hidden Agenda," *National Review Online*, August 28, 2009. Reproduced by permission.

As you read, consider the following questions:

1. What does Andrew C. McCarthy say that Barack Obama and Eric Holder promised their anti-war base during the 2008 campaign?

2. What part of the Geneva Conventions does McCarthy maintain the United States has rejected?

3. How would international arrest warrants affect indicted U.S. officials, according to McCarthy?

"This is an administration that is determined to conduct itself by the rule of law. And to the extent that we receive lawful requests from an appropriately created court, we would obviously respond to it."

It was springtime [2009] in Berlin and Eric Holder, a well-known "rule of law" devotee, was speaking to the German press. He'd been asked if his Justice Department would cooperate with efforts by foreign or international tribunals to prosecute U.S. government officials who carried out the [George W.] Bush administration's post-9/11 [after the terrorist attacks of September 11, 2001] counterterrorism policies. The attorney general assured listeners that he was certainly open to being helpful. "Obviously," he said, "we would look at any request that would come from a court in any country and see how and whether we should comply with it."

As the Associated Press reported at the time, Holder was "pressed on whether that meant the United States would cooperate with a foreign court prosecuting Bush administration officials." He skirted the question in a way Americans ought to find alarming. The attorney general indicated that he was speaking only about "evidentiary requests." Translation: The [Barack] Obama administration will not make arrests and hand current or former American government officials over for foreign trials, but if the Europeans or U.N. [United Nations] functionaries (at the nudging of, say, the Organization of the Islamic Conference[1]) want Justice's help gathering evidence in order to build triable cases—count us in.

Investigations on Behalf of Internationalism

Hue and cry followed Holder's decision this week [August 2009] to have a prosecutor investigate CIA [Central Intelligence Agency] interrogators and contractors. The probe is a nakedly political, banana republic-style criminalizing of policy differences and political rivalry. The abuse allegations said to have stunned the attorney general into acting are outlined in a stale CIA inspector general's report. Though only released this week—a disclosure timed to divert attention from reports that showed the CIA's efforts yielded life-saving intelligence—the IG [Inspector General] report is actually five years old. Its allegations not only have been long known to the leaders of both parties in Congress, they were thoroughly investigated by professional prosecutors—not political appointees. Those prosecutors decided not to file charges, except in one case that ended in an acquittal. . . . The abuse in question falls woefully short of torture crimes under federal law.

Americans are scratching their heads: Why would Holder retrace this well-worn ground when intimidating our intelligence-gatherers so obviously damages national security? The political fallout, too, is palpable. Leon Panetta, the outraged CIA director, is reportedly pondering resignation. President Obama, laying low in the tall grass on his Martha's Vineyard vacation, is having staffers try to put distance between himself and his attorney general. It is unlikely that many will be fooled: Both Obama and Holder promised their antiwar base just this sort of "reckoning" during the 2008 campaign [for President]. But the question remains, Why is Holder (or, rather, why are Holder and the White House) instigating this controversy?

1. The Organization of the Islamic Conference is an organization of more than 50 member states with majority Muslim populations. It has a permanent delegation to the United Nations.

I believe the explanation lies in the Obama administration's fondness for transnationalism, a doctrine of post-sovereign globalism in which America is seen as owing its principal allegiance to the international legal order rather than to our own Constitution and national interests.

Recall that the president chose to install former Yale Law School dean Harold Koh as his State Department's legal adviser. Koh is the country's leading proponent of transnationalism. He is now a major player in the administration's deliberations over international law and cooperation. Naturally, membership in the International Criminal Court, which the United States has resisted joining, is high on Koh's agenda. The ICC claims worldwide jurisdiction, even over nations that do not ratify its enabling treaty, notwithstanding that sovereign consent to jurisdiction is a bedrock principle of international law.

The Danger of International Law

As a result, there have always been serious concerns that the ICC could investigate and try to indict American political, military, and intelligence officials for actions taken in defense of our country. Here it's crucial to bear in mind that the United States (or at least the pre-Obama United States) has not seen eye-to-eye with Europe on significant national-security matters. European nations, for example, have accepted the 1977 Protocol I to the Geneva Conventions,[2] while the United States has rejected it. Protocol I extends protections to terrorists and imposes an exacting legal regime on combat operations, relying on such concepts as "proportional" use of force and rigorous distinction between military and civilian targets. That is, Protocol I potentially converts traditional combat operations into war crimes. Similarly, though the U.S. accepted the torture provisions of the U.N. Convention Against

2. The Geneva Conventions are international laws governing the conduct of states in wartime.

Torture (UNCAT), our nation rejected the UNCAT's placing of "cruel, inhuman, and degrading treatment" on a par with torture. By contrast, Europe generally accepts the UNCAT in toto.

As long as we haven't ratified a couple of bad human-rights treaties, why should we care that Europe considers them binding? Because of the monstrosity known as "customary international law," of which Koh is a major proponent. This theory holds that once new legal principles gain broad acceptance among nations and international organizations, they somehow transmogrify into binding law, even for nations that haven't agreed to them. That is, the judgment of the "international community" (meaning, the judgment of left-wing academics and human-rights activists who hold sway at the U.N. and the European Union) supersedes the standards our citizens have adopted democratically. It is standard fare among transnational progressives to claim that Protocol I is now binding on the United States and that what they define as cruel, inhuman, and degrading treatment is "tantamount to torture."

And the transnational Left has still another treat in store: its notion of "universal jurisdiction." This theory holds that individual nations have the power to prosecute actions that occur in other countries, even when they have no impact on the prosecuting nation. The idea is that some offenses—such as torture and war crimes—so offend the purported consensus of humanity (i.e., so offend left-wing sensibilities) that they may be prosecuted by any country that cares to take the initiative. In fact, many countries (the United States included) open their justice systems to civil suits against government officials—again, even if the country where the suit is filed has nothing to do with the alleged offenses.

Holder's Plot

So we come back to Holder in Berlin. Two months before the attorney general's visit, the U.N.'s "special rapporteur on tor-

Protocol I

It is surely no coincidence that many of the states which have not ratified the protocol [that is, Protocol I of the Geneva Conventions, which modified the international law of war, particularly in relation to treatment of irregular forces and civilians] are confronted by genuine threat, or actual existence, of an international armed conflict. . . .

It would be grossly dismissive and reductionist to tar the non-ratifying states with the brush of lack of respect for civilian life. . . . Rather, it must simply [be] the case that these states . . . to believe adherence to Additional Protocol I would make the successful execution of military action difficult or impossible.

David McGrogan,
"Whither Now, Additional Protocol I?"
International Law Observer, January 31, 2009.
http://internationallawobserver.eu.

ture" told German television that the Obama administration had "a clear obligation" under the UNCAT to file torture charges against former president George W. Bush and former defense secretary Donald Rumsfeld. The rapporteur was relying on documents produced because of American investigations—including a nakedly partisan report by the Democrat-controlled Senate Armed Services Committee.

Meanwhile, . . . in March [2009], Spain's universal-justice crusader Baltasar Garzón is pursuing his own torture case against Bush administration lawyers who weighed in on interrogation policy. Garzón is the Spanish investigating magistrate who, with the help of a terrorist turned human-rights lawyer, had Chilean strongman Augusto Pinochet arrested in England for crimes against humanity. The same terrorist-lawyer, Gonzalo Boye, is helping Garzón on the Bush case. The Brits, by the way, eventually decided not to send Pinochet to Spain, but not before the law lords ruled that they could, a decision enthusiastically hailed at the time by U.N. High Commissioner on Human Rights Mary Robinson, the former president of Ireland. That would be the same Mary Robinson of Durban infamy—the one President Obama just honored with the Medal of Freedom.[3]

And then there is the Center for Constitutional Rights [CCR]; a Marxist organization[4] that for years has coordinated legal representation for terrorists detained at Guantanamo Bay [Cuba]. The CCR has been attempting to convince Germany, France, Spain, and other countries to file war-crime indictments against former Bush admiration officials, including President Bush, Vice President [Dick] Cheney, and Secretary [of Defense Donald] Rumsfeld. In representing America's enemies, CCR has collaborated with many private lawyers, who also volunteered their services—several of whom are now working in the Obama Justice Department. Indeed, Holder's former firm boasts that it still represents 16 Gitmo[5] detainees (the number was previously higher). And, for help shaping detainee policy, Holder recently hired Jennifer Daskal for DOJ [Department of Justice]'s National Security Division—a lawyer from Human Rights Watch with no prior prosecutorial experience, whose main qualification seems to be the startling advocacy she has done for enemy combatants.[6]

Put it all together and it's really not that hard to figure out what is going on here.

---

3. Mary Robinson presided over the 2001 World Conference Against Racism. The conference was accused of anti-semitic bias by the United States and Israel.
4. CCR was co-founded by William Kunstler. Kunstler describes himself as a radical, though the center itself is not avowedly Marxist.
5. Gitmo is an abbreviation of Guantanamo Bay Naval Base.
6. Jennifer Daskal has argued that the Bush Administration tortured detainees, and that some accused detainees were innocent.

Hoping for International Prosecutions

Transnationalists from outside and, now, inside our government have been ardent supporters of prosecutions against American officials who designed and carried out the Bush counterterrorism policies that kept this country safe after 9/11. The U.N.'s top torture monitor is demanding legal action, almost certainly as a prelude to calling for action by an international tribunal—such as the ICC [International Criminal Court]—if the Justice Department fails to indict. Meantime, law-enforcement authorities in Spain and elsewhere are weighing charges against the same U.S. officials, spurred on by the CCR and human-rights groups that now have friends in high American places. In foreign and international courts, the terrorist-friendly legal standards preferred by Europe and the U.N. would make convictions easier to obtain and civil suits easier to win.

Obama and Holder were principal advocates for a "reckoning" against Bush officials during the 2008 campaign. They realize, though, that their administration would be mortally wounded if Justice were actually to file formal charges—this week's announcement of an investigation against the CIA provoked howls, but that's nothing compared to the public reaction indictments would cause. Nevertheless, Obama and Holder are under intense pressure from the hard Left, to which they made reckless promises, and from the international community they embrace.

The way out of this dilemma is clear. Though it won't file indictments against the CIA agents and Bush officials it is probing, the Justice Department will continue conducting investigations and releasing reports containing new disclosures of information. The churn of new disclosures will be used by lawyers for the detainees to continue pressing the U.N. and the Europeans to file charges. The European nations and/or international tribunals will make formal requests to the Obama administration to have the Justice Department assist them in securing evidence. Holder will piously announce that the "rule of law" requires him to cooperate with these "lawful requests" from "appropriately created courts." Finally, the international and/or foreign courts will file criminal charges against American officials.

Foreign charges would result in the issuance of international arrest warrants. They won't be executed in the United States—even this administration is probably not brazen enough to try that. But the warrants will go out to police agencies all over the world. If the indicted American officials want to travel outside the U.S., they will need to worry about the possibility of arrest, detention, and transfer to third countries for prosecution. . . . CCR president Michael Ratner . . . brags that his European gambit is "making the world smaller" for Rumsfeld—creating a hostile legal climate in which a former U.S. defense secretary may have to avoid, for instance, attending conferences in NATO countries.

The Left will get its reckoning. Obama and Holder will be able to take credit with their supporters for making it happen. But because the administration's allies in the antiwar bar and the international Left will do the dirty work of getting charges filed, the American media will help Obama avoid domestic political accountability. Meanwhile, Americans who sought to protect our nation from barbarians will be harassed and framed as war criminals. And protecting the United States will have become an actionable violation of international law.

I'm betting that's the plan.

Periodical Bibliography

The following articles have been selected to supplement the diverse views presented in this chapter.

John Byrne — "U.S. Violated Geneva Conventions, Bush Iraq Commander Says," *AlterNet*, May 30, 2009. www.alternet.org.

Marjorie Cohn — "Donald Rumsfeld: The War Crimes Case," *JURIST*, November 9, 2006. http://jurist.law.pitt.edu.

Alan M. Dershowitz — "The Rules of War Enable Terror," *aish.com*, June 5, 2004.

Reuel Marc Gerecht — "Out of Sight," *New York Times*, December 13, 2008. www.nytimes.com.

Thomas C. Goldstein and Cody S. Harris — "Foreign Law and Constitutional Interpretation: The Debate Behind the Diatribes," American Enterprise Institute Web site, August 20, 2009. www.aei.org.

Julian G. Ku — "The President's Unexamined Power to Interpret Customary International Law," American Enterprise Institute Web site, August 20, 2009. www.aei.org.

Jason Leopold — "Detainees Were Also Murdered at Bagram in Afghanistan," *Antemedius*, June 25, 2009. www.antemedius.com.

Ewan McAskill — "Guantánamo 'Is Within Geneva Conventions,'" *The Guardian*, February 21, 2009. www.guardian.co.uk.

Pejman Yousefzadeh — "International Law and Torture Memos," *New Ledger*, April 17, 2009. www.newledger.com.

For Further Discussion

Chapter 1

1. Which of the viewpoints in this chapter does not use the word torture? What phrase does the author use instead? Why do you think this author is unwilling to use the term "torture"?

2. In his discussion of torture, Glenn Greenwald argues that there is no reasonable argument to be made on behalf of torturing those captured in the war on terror. Do you think Ross Douthat, Jonah Goldberg, or Oren Gross provide reasonable arguments explaining why torture may sometimes be necessary or at least excusable?

Chapter 2

1. Claudio Ochoa discusses the case *United States v. Reynolds*, in which the state secrets privilege was clarified. How does Ochoa's account of the facts in the *Reynolds* case differ from the facts of the case discussed by Henry Lanman? After reading both accounts, do you think the government should have been allowed to invoke the state secrets privilege in this case?

2. Based on the argument in Andrew C. McCarthy's viewpoint, is there any law that the president could not break during a wartime emergency?

Chapter 3

1. David Barron et al., argue that there is nothing wrong with signing statements in themselves; problems arise, however, when the president actually fails to enforce a law. Does Robert Justin Lipkin agree, or does he believe that signing statements themselves raise constitutional questions? Explain your answer.

Chapter 4

1. Do Niles Gardiner and James Jay Carafano admit the existence of secret U.S. prisons at which torture has occurred? Based on their argument, can you tell whether they would defend such practices if they did occur?

2. According to Sangitha McKenzie Millar, extraordinary rendition violates U.S. law as well as international law. Do you think Andrew C. McCarthy would agree with the prosecution of George W. Bush administration officials under domestic law? Why or why not?

3. Jan Frel compares George W. Bush's actions in invading Iraq to the atrocities committed by Nazi Germany during the Holocaust. Do you find his argument convincing? Do you think the comparison to the Nazis helps or hurts his case that Bush should be tried for war crimes?

Organizations to Contact

The editors have compiled the following list of organizations concerned with the issues debated in this book. The descriptions are derived from materials provided by the organizations. All have publications or information available for interested readers. The list was compiled on the date of publication of the present volume; the information provided here may change. Be aware that many organizations take several weeks or longer to respond to inquiries, so allow as much time as possible.

American Civil Liberties Union (ACLU)
125 Broad St., 18th Fl., New York, NY   10004
(212) 549-2585
Web site: www.aclu.org

Founded in 1920, the ACLU is a national organization that works to defend civil liberties in the United States. It publishes regular in-depth reports, the newsletter *Civil Liberties*, and a set of handbooks on individual rights. Its Web site includes "The Torture Report," an effort to give a full account of the George W. Bush administration's torture record based on government documents, investigations, press reports, witness accounts, and other sources. The ACLU Web site also regularly publishes updates and news related to civil liberties and abuse of executive authority, such as "Justice Denied Video: Voices from Guantanamo," and "ACLU Obtains More Documents Related to Bush Admin Torture Program."

American Enterprise Institute for Public Policy Research (AEI)
1150 17th St. NW, Washington, DC   20036
(202) 862-5800 • fax: (202) 862-7177
Web site: www.aei.org

AEI is a conservative research and education organization that studies national and international issues, including political and public opinion studies. It is committed to expanding liberty, increasing individual opportunity, and strengthening free enterprise. The institute publishes the monthly periodicals *American Enterprise* and *AEI Economist*, and the bimonthly *Public Opinion*. The Web site includes such articles and policy papers as "Vital Presidential Power."

Amnesty International USA (AI)

5 Penn Plaza, New York, NY 10001
(212) 807-8400 • fax: (212) 627-1451
e-mail: aimember@aiusa.org
Web site: www.amnestyusa.org

This international organization works to promote human rights around the world. Amnesty International USA posts updates on human rights issues on its Web site, which includes reports on U.S. human rights issues, such as "USA: President Obama Defends Guantanamo Closure, But Endorses 'War' Paradigm and Indefinite Preventive Detention," and "USA Concern for Mental Health of Guantanamo Detainee Held Since He Was 17 Years Old."

Brookings Institution

1775 Massachusetts Ave. NW, Washington, DC 20036
(202) 797-6000
e-mail: www.brookings.edu/about/contactUs.aspx
Web site: www.brookings.edu

The Brookings Institution, founded in 1927, is a liberal think tank that conducts research and education in foreign policy, economics, government, and the social sciences. It publishes the quarterly *Brookings Review*, the biannual *Brookings Papers on Economic Activity*, and various books, including *Power Play: The Bush Presidency and the Constitution*.

Cato Institute

1000 Massachusetts Ave. NW, Washington, DC 20001-5403
(202) 842-0200 • fax: (202) 842-3490
Web site: www.cato.org

The Cato Institute is a libertarian public policy research foundation dedicated to increasing the understanding of public policies based on the principles of limited government, free markets, individual liberty, and peace. It publishes the triannual *Cato Journal*, the periodic *Cato Policy Analysis*, and a bimonthly newsletter, *Cato Policy Review*. The Web site also includes articles, such as "Conservatives and the Presidency," and multimedia presentations such as a video and podcast of the lecture "Obama and Presidential Power: Change or Continuity?"

Center for American Progress

1333 H St. NW, 10th Fl., Washington, DC   20005
(202) 682-1611 • fax: (202) 682-1867
e-mail: progress@americanprogress.org
Web site: www.americanprogress.org/

The Center for American Progress is a progressive think tank with an interest in values such as diversity, shared and personal responsibility, and participatory government. It publishes broadly on economic issues, including business regulation, credit and debt, the global economy, health care, immigration, and the environment. The Web site includes articles and reports, such as "Five Steps to Close Guantanamo," and "Government Secrecy on the Rise."

Common Cause

1133 19th St. NW, 9th Fl., Washington, DC   20036
(202) 833-1200
Web site: www.commoncause.org

Common Cause is a nonprofit, nonpartisan, advocacy group, founded in 1970, to hold elected leaders accountable to the American people. Common Cause pushes for tighter ethics regulations and more open government. The organization has chapters in thirty-six states. Its Web site has an archive of its online journal, *Common Cause Magazine*. The Web site also includes information about the organization's initiatives, such as its advocacy for a truth and reconciliation commission, and for the official commendation of those in government who worked to stop torture. The Web site also provides informational pages on rule of law issues, including "Torture and Secret Prisons," and "Signing Statements."

Heritage Foundation

214 Massachusetts Ave. NE, Washington, DC   20002-4999
(202) 546-4400 • fax: (202) 546-8328
e-mail: info@heritage.org
Web site: www.heritage.org

The Heritage Foundation is a conservative public policy research institute dedicated to the principles of free, competitive enterprise, limited government, and individual liberty. Its scholars write numerous articles on politics and the party system. Among its publications are the periodic *Backgrounder* and the monthly *Policy Review*. The organization's Web site also offers numerous articles and policy position papers, including "Energy in the Executive: Re-examining Presidential Power in the Midst of the War on Terrorism," and "War Time Presidential Power Presents Constitutional Dilemma."

Human Rights Watch (HRW)

350 Fifth Ave., 34th Fl., New York, NY   10118-3299
(212) 290-4700 • fax: (212) 736-1300
e-mail: hrwnyc@hrw.org
Web site: www.hrw.org

Human Rights Watch is a nonprofit, nongovernmental human rights organization made up of more than 275 staff members worldwide, including country experts, lawyers, journalists, and academics. The organization publishes numerous books and policy papers, sponsors an annual film festival on human rights issues, and files lawsuits on behalf of those who believe their rights have been violated. Its Web site includes various reports, such as "Fighting Terrorism Fairly: Recommendations for President Obama."

Reason Foundation

3415 S Sepulveda Blvd., Suite 400, Los Angeles, CA   90034
(310) 391-2245 • fax: (310) 391-4395

The Reason Foundation promotes individual freedoms and free-market principles. It contends that the United States should avoid the extremes of isolationism and interventionism in its foreign policy. Publications include the monthly *Reason* magazine (which includes Web-only content at *Reason Online*), newsletters, research reports, and books. The Web site also offers numerous articles, such as "President of Everything," and "Where Did Bush Go Wrong?"

Bibliography of Books

Books

Mirko Bagaric
and Julie Clarke

Torture: When the Unthinkable Is Morally Permissible. Albany, NY: State University of New York Press, 2007.

Bob Brecher

Torture and the Ticking Bomb. Malden, MA: Blackwell Publishing, 2007.

Vincent Bugliosi

The Prosecution of George W. Bush for Murder. Cambridge, MA: Perseus Books, 2008.

Steven G. Calabresi and Christopher S. Yoo

The Unitary Executive: Presidential Power from Washington to Bush. New Haven, CT: Yale University Press, 2008.

Mark Danner

Torture and Truth: America, Abu Ghraib, and the War on Terror. New York: New York Review of Books, 2004.

Karen J. Greenberg

The Torture Debate in America. New York: Cambridge University Press, 2006.

Oren Gross and Fionnuala Ní Aoláin

Law in Times of Crisis: Emergency Powers in Theory and Practice. New York: Cambridge University Press, 2006.

Michael Hass	*George W. Bush, War Criminal? The Administration's Liability for 269 War Crimes.* Westport, CT: Praegar Publishers, 2009.
Robert G. Kaufman	*In Defense of the Bush Doctrine.* Lexington, KY: University Press of Kentucky, 2007.
Mark R. Levin	*Liberty and Tyranny.* New York: Threshold Editions, 2009.
Sanford Levinson	*Torture: A Collection.* New York: Oxford University Press, 2004.
Dennis Loo and Peter Phillips, eds.	*Impeach the President: The Case Against Bush and Cheney.* New York: Seven Stories Press, 2006.
John P. Mackenzie	*Absolute Power: How the Unitary Executive Theory Is Undermining the Constitution.* New York: Century Foundation Press, 2008.
Thomas E. Mann and Norman J. Ornstein	*The Broken Branch: How Congress Is Failing America and How to Get It Back on Track.* New York: Oxford University Press, 2008.
Joseph Margulies	*Guantanamo and the Abuse of Presidential Power.* New York: Simon & Schuster, 2006.
Jane Mayer	*The Dark Side: The Inside Story of How the War on Terror Turned into a War on American Ideals.* New York: Doubleday, 2008.

Richard E.
Neustadt

Presidential Power and the Modern President: The Politics of Leadership from Roosevelt to Reagan. New York: Free Press, 1990.

Barbara
Olshansky

Democracy Detained: Secret Unconstitutional Practices in the U.S. War on Terror. New York: Seven Stories Press, 2007.

Richard Posner

Not a Suicide Pact: The Constitution in a Time of National Emergency. New York: Oxford University Press, 2006.

Darius Rejali

Torture and Democracy. New Haven, CT: Yale University Press, 2009.

Andrew
Rudalevige

The New Imperial Presidency: Renewing Presidential Power After Watergate. Ann Arbor, MI: University of Michigan Press, 2006.

Philippe Sands

Torture Team: Rumsfeld's Memo and the Betrayal of American Values. New York: Palgrave Macmillan, 2008.

Frederick A.O.
Schwarz Jr. and
Azis Z. Huq

Unchecked and Unbalanced: Presidential Power in a Time of Terror. New York: New Press, 2008.

Robert Y. Shapiro,
Martha Joynt
Kumar, and
Lawrence R.
Jacobs

Presidential Power. New York: Columbia University Press, 2000.

John Yoo   *Crisis and Command: A History of Executive Power from George Washington to George W. Bush*. New York: Kaplan Publishing, 2010.

John Yoo   *The Powers of War and Peace: The Constitution and Foreign Affairs After 9/11*. Chicago, IL: University of Chicago Press, 2006.

Index

A

ABA (American Bar Association), 118–124

Abramowitz, Michael, 170

Abu Ghraib detention center (Iraq)

photographs of prisoners, 38, 49

sadism by prison guards, 27–28

torture of prisoners, 14–16, 49–50, 151

See also Iraq war

Accountability for torture, 78

Greenwald's call for, 16

Gross's call for, 73

legislation related to, 65

Obama's call for, 85

opposition to, 66

Rumsfeld's call for, 14

Accountability of presidents

reasons against, 204–212

reasons for, 197–203

Addicott, Jeffrey, 134–139

Afghanistan

Congressional approval for war in, 106

failed state status, 159–160

Geneva Conventions and, 154, 156, 161

military sweeps in, 43

prisoners captured in, 164, 169, 178

Salt Pit torture site, 180

Taliban government in, 136, 153–154, 158, 160, 164, 169

terrorist training camps, 23, 175

torture dogs trained in, 52

U.S. invasion of, 15

al-Qaeda terrorist group

Geneva Conventions and, 157–158

New York Times article on, 25

9/11 attack by, 21–23

plots developed by, 36–37

Terrorist Surveillance Program vs., 24–25

threats to U.S. values, 79

waterboarding members of, 54

See also bin Laden, Osama; Khan, A.Q.; Mohammed, Khalid Sheikh; War on Terror; Zubaydah, Abu

al-Shaykh al-Libi, Ibn (al-Qaeda leader), 42

American Bar Association (ABA), 118–124

American Bar Association (ABA) Task Force, 121, 123, 125–126

American Civil Liberties Union (ACLU), 84–85, 100, 141

"The American Prospect" essay (Podesta), 83

Anthrax attacks, 23, 36

Article Two (II) (U.S. Constitution), 24, 92, 120, 155, 158–160, 165, 172

Ashcroft, John, 83

Associated Press-Ipsos poll, 72

Atlantic magazine essay, 49, 55

Atomic bombing of Japan, 52–53